D0615848

Education for Choosing Life

Cardinal Jorge Mario Bergoglio, S.J.

Education
for Choosing Life

Proposals for Difficult Times

Translation by Deborah Cole

IGNATIUS PRESS   SAN FRANCISCO

Originally published in Spanish as
Educar, Elegir la Vida:
Propuestas para tiempos difíciles
© 2005 by Editorial Claretiana
Buenos Aires, Argentina

Cover photograph by
Stefano Spaziani

Cover design by Roxanne Mei Lum

© 2014 by Ignatius Press, San Francisco
All rights reserved
ISBN 978-1-58617-890-1
Library of Congress Control Number 2013955220
Printed in the United States of America ∞

Contents

Foreword

How long can we walk without a defined path? How can we arrive when there is no goal to guide our steps? What can we propose if we don't know who we are? The use of the plural in these questions is not an accident. Because, while it is certainly true that in some way they sum up the anxieties of the human heart, they also express the future of a people in the process of building their identity.

And it is times of crisis that truly reveal what we are made of. They urgently rouse the voices that restore meaning to uncertain wandering.

In this framework we present the messages of Cardinal Bergoglio to educational communities in the last three years, along with proposals for their implementation at the personal and group level.

The words of the archbishop of Buenos Aires reveal a man of God who, for this very reason, is profoundly committed to the destiny of his fellows. They are words that invite us to recall our roots, to turn our gaze toward the values of our people, to renew our confidence in the true richness of our country. And in this sense, they synthesize and stimulate the task which has for some time been in progress in the Vicarage of Education of the Archdiocese.

In the first of the messages, the pastor addresses the world of education in order to remind us that "far from being a mere consoling fantasy, an imaginary flight of evasion, utopia is a form that hope assumes in a concrete historical situation." Thus, the hinge of his reflection invites us to live in "creativity as a characteristic of active hope".

At the beginning of the second message, he states: "If we look at Jesus, incarnate Wisdom of God, we can realize that difficulties become challenges, challenges appeal to hope and generate the happiness of recognizing them as architects of something new. All this undoubtedly drives us to continue giving the best of ourselves." An entire plan for life.

In the third message, the cardinal invites educators to reflect on "the task of *accompanying children and young people in the process of their maturation*". He affirms that "it is essential to try to approach the reality lived by our youth in our society, and ask ourselves what role we play in it." He calls for establishing concrete goals for education in maturity.

Broad horizons, solid fraternity, and going even further, efficacious generosity, the excellence of solidarity, are original concepts that the cardinal promotes as a part of our specifically Christian contribution to an education that witnesses to and brings about another way of being human.

"Our objective is not only to form individuals who are useful to society but to educate persons who can transform it! . . . Either we are capable of forming men and women with this mentality, or we will have failed in our mission."

The path is defined. Now we can walk.

—The Editor
Editorial Claretiana

1

Being Creative, for an Active Hope

An Act of Hope

Exactly one year ago, I began my message to the educational communities talking about a critical and decisive moment in the life of our people. Many things have happened since then: suffering, confusion, indignation, but also plenty of putting the shoulder to the wheel on the part of so many men and women who offered themselves to their neighbors without trying to justify indifference or wanting to "save themselves" from others. In sum, we find ourselves with the conviction that we must not hope for any *savior*, any *magical* decision that will urge us forward or make us fulfill our "true destiny". There is no *true destiny*; there is no magic. What exists is a people with a history that is full of questioning and doubts, with institutions that are barely maintaining themselves, with values that are followed by a question mark, with minimal short-term tools. These things are too weighty to be entrusted to a charismatic leader or a technician, things that can work their way to a happier outcome only by means of *a collective action of historic creation*. And I do not think I am mistaken in my intuition that your task as educators is going to be in the *vanguard* of this challenge. To create collectively a better reality, with the limits and possibilities of history, is *an act of hope*. Not of certainties, not of mere wagers:

neither destiny nor chance. It demands beliefs and virtues. To put in play every resource, in addition to an incalculable "something" that gives it its drama.

This year's reflection also bears *on hope*, but most in particular on an essential component of its active dimension: *creativity*. Because if we are in a moment of historic and collective creation, our task as educators can no longer be limited to "keep doing what we're doing", nor even "to resist" in the face of a supremely adverse reality: it is a matter of creating, of beginning to put in place the bricks of a new edifice in the middle of history, that is to say, located in a present that has a past and—let us hope—also a future.

Utopia and Historic Creation

For us, to talk about *creation* has an immediate connotation of belief. Faith in God the Creator tells us that the history of mankind is not an endless void: it has a beginning and also a direction. The God who created "heaven and earth" is the same who made a promise to a people, and his absolute power is a guarantee of the efficacy of his Love. *Faith in creation, in this way, is a foundation of hope.* Human history, our history, the history of each of us, of our families, of our communities, the concrete history that we construct day by day in our schools, is never *finished*, never exhausts its possibilities, but can always open to the new, to what until now had not been considered, to what had seemed impossible. This is so because that history forms a part of a creation that has its roots in the power and the love of God.

Once more, it is appropriate to clarify that this is not a matter of a kind of official balance between pessimism and optimism. We are talking about *hope*, and hope does not feel comfortable with either of these two options. Let us center ourselves in *creativity as a characteristic of an active hope*. In what sense can we be creative, creators, we human beings? It will not be in the sense of *creating out of nothing* like God, obviously. Our capacity to create is much more humble and limited since it is a gift of God that, before everything else, we must receive. At the moment of exercising our creativity, we must learn to move ourselves within *the tension between innovation and continuity*. That is to say, we must open the way for the new starting from the known. For human creativity, there is neither *creation ex nihil* nor *identical repetition of the same thing*. To act creatively implies to take into serious account what there is, in all its density, and to find the way by which from that starting point something new may become manifest.

At this point, we can once again invoke, as we did last year, one of the most important masters of the faith: *Saint Augustine*. In his work *The City of God*, this Father of the Church reflected on the *sense of history* from the perspective of *eschatological salvation* accomplished in Christ. The imminent fall of the Roman Empire announced a profound historical change: the end of one epoch and the uncertain beginning of another. Saint Augustine determined to understand the designs of God in order to illuminate a Church that had been entrusted to his ministry. We have already laid out the central elements of this work in last year's message. Ultimately, we referred to *human history as a place of discernment between offerings of grace* which were oriented toward the full realization of man, society, and history in eschatological redemption, and *temptations to sin*, trying to construct a future in opposition to the divine dynamic of salvation.

But there are other dimensions of this Augustinian thought that can orient us in the search for historical creativity. To take advantage of his teaching, it is necessary above all to ask ourselves about the *meaning of utopia*. In the first place, utopias are the fruit of the imagination, the projection toward the future of a constellation of desires and aspirations. Utopia takes its strength from two elements: on the one hand, the disagreement, the dissatisfaction or malaise that present reality provokes; on the other, the unbreakable conviction that another world is possible. Its mobilizing force springs from this. Far from being a mere consoling fantasy, an imaginary alienation, *utopia is a form that hope takes in a concrete historical situation.*

The belief that the world is perfectible and that the human person has resources to attain a fuller life nourishes all utopian construction. But this belief goes hand in hand with the concrete search for interventions to make this ideal realizable. Because if indeed the term *utopia* literally refers to something "in no place", something that does not exist in a localizable way, neither does it point to a complete estrangement from historic reality. On the contrary, it aims at a possible development, although imaginary for the moment. Let us make a note of this: something that does not yet exist, *something new, but which it is necessary to move toward, starting from that which is.* In that way, every utopia includes a description of an ideal society, but also an analysis of the mechanisms or strategies that could make it possible. We would say that it is a projection toward the future that tends to turn toward the present searching its avenues of possibility, in this order: first, the ideal, delineated vividly; then, certain interventions that hypothetically would make it viable.

But in addition, in its *to-and-fro* as it departs from the present, it is supported fundamentally in the *negation of the nondesirable aspects of present reality*. It emerges from the rejection (not visceral but intellectual) of a situation considered as bad, unjust, dehumanizing, alienating, and so forth. In that sense, it is necessary to point out that utopia proposes the new . . . but without ever freeing itself from the actual. It outlines the expectation of a change from the present perception of what would be desirable if we could free ourselves of the factors that oppress us, from the tendencies that impede us from yielding to something superior. From two distinct directions, then, we see the *indissoluble connection between the desired future and the tolerated present*. Utopia is not pure fantasy: it is also a critique of reality and a search for new paths.

In that rejection of the present in pursuit of another possible world, expressed as a leap to the future which must subsequently find its paths in order to become viable, there are *two serious limits*: first, a certain *"mad" quality*, proper to its fantastic or imaginary character, which can change it into a mere dream, an impossible desire, if this dimension is accentuated rather than the practical aspects of its construction. Something of this resonates in certain current usage of the term. The second limit: in its rejection of the present and desire to establish something new, it can fall into an even more ferocious and intransigent *authoritarianism* than that which it wanted to overcome. How many utopian ideals in the history of mankind have not yielded to every kind of injustice, intolerance, persecution, abuse, and dictatorship of different kinds?

Now then: it is precisely these two limits of utopian thought that have provoked its *discredit* at the present time; either because of a supposed realism which is attached to *the possible*, understanding that possible as the sole play of the dominant forces, rejecting the human capacity to create reality from an ethical aspiration; or because of surfeit in the face of promises of certain new worlds which, in the last century, have brought only more suffering to the people.

And here we can return to the reading of *The City of God*. Utopia, such as we know it, is a typically modern construction (if indeed it is rooted in millenarian movements that cut across the second half of the Middle Ages). But Saint Augustine, setting out his outline of the "two cities" (the City of God, ruled by love, and the earthly city, by egoism) inextricably juxtaposed in secular history, offers us some *keys for pinning down the relation between change and continuity*, which is precisely the *critical point of utopian thought and the key to all historical creativity*. Indeed, *The City of God* is, in the first place, a *criticism of the concept that worshiped political power and the status quo*. And this was not only a question of the *pagans*; once Christianity was adopted as the religion of Imperial Rome, it began defining an *official theology* that sustained this political reality as if it were already the Kingdom of God consummated upon earth.

It was just this type of theological reading of a historical reality that Augustine opposed in his work. By showing the seeds of corruption in imperial Rome, he was breaking any identification between the Kingdom of Christ and the kingdom of this world. And presenting the City of God as a present reality in history, but mixed with the earthly City and only *separable* in the final Judgment, he made room for the possibility of the *other possible history*, lived and constructed by other values and other ideals. If in the *official theology* history was the exclusive and exclusionary place of self-referential power, in the City of God there is established a space for liberty which embraces the gift of salvation and the divine project of a transfigured mankind and world. A project that will be consummated in the eschaton, it is true, but which already in history can be gestating new realities, overthrowing false determinisms, opening again and again the horizon of hope and of creativity of an *enrichment* of meaning, of a promise that is always inviting one to forge ahead.

We can also come to terms with *the "utopian" moment from its criticism of consecrated models*, and link it to the *realism* with which the bishop of Hippo considered his active membership in the Church. Because another aspect of our saint is his committed and concrete struggle for the construction of a Church that is strong, united, centered in an experience of faith of which he himself was a privileged witness, but also achieved in an historical and earthly manner in a concrete community. His firm position vis-à-vis the Donatists (a current that claimed a Church of the pure, without room for sinners) brought to light the realistic conviction that the hope of a new heaven and a new earth must not leave us with our arms crossed in the face of today's challenges, in pursuit of a purity or noncontamination of the earthly, but rather—on the contrary—it must give us an orientation and the selfsame energy to gather the daily clay, the ambiguous clay from which human history is made, in order to capture a world more worthy of the daughters and sons of God. Not heaven on earth: only *a more human world*, awaiting the eschatological action of God.

Historical creativity, then, from the Christian perspective, is governed by the parable of the wheat and the tares. It is necessary to project utopias, and at the same time it is necessary to take account of what is. The option of "erase and start over" does not exist. To be creative is not to throw overboard everything that constitutes the present reality, as limited, corrupt, and worn out as it may be. There is no future without the present and without the past: creativity also implies memory and discernment, equanimity and justice, prudence, and strength. If we are going to try to bring something to our homeland from the field of education, we cannot lose sight of both poles: the utopian and the realistic, because both are an integral part of historical creativity. We must look forward to the new but not throw in the trash what others (and even we ourselves) have built with effort.

A Creative One in Argentine History

Let us attempt to see this in a way that is a little more concrete. Now that we are on the subject, why not try to allow ourselves to be instructed by history? Thinking about the founding time of our country, I set out in search of a personage whose relevance to the emerging Argentina is not generally recognized. I refer to *Manuel Belgrano*.

What can we say about him, in addition to his participation in the First Junta and the creation of the flag? He was not a *successful* man, at least in the terms in which we are accustomed to using that word at this present time of pragmatism and nonsense. His military campaigns lacked the brilliance and profundity that gained the title of *Liberator* for José de San Martín. He lacked the pen of the writer and propagandist like Sarmiento. As a politician, he was always relegated to second rank. His private life, too, was not particularly noteworthy: his health left something to be desired, he could not marry the woman he loved, and he died at the age of fifty, in poverty. Nevertheless, Sarmiento said of him that he had been "one of the very few who did not have to beg pardon of posterity and of the severe critic, history. His obscure death is still a guarantee that he was an upstanding citizen, a faultless patriot." The same could be said for very few of the *successful* in our national history. It is that in addition to his insuperable personal virtues and his profound Christian faith, Belgrano was a man who, at the right moment, knew how to find the dynamism, drive, and equilibrium that define true creativity: the difficult but fertile conjunction of realistic continuity and generous change. His influence in the dawn of our national identity is much greater than is supposed; and for that reason it can once again arise in order to show us, in this time of uncertainty but also of challenge, *how to go about* laying firm foundations in an enterprise of historic creation.

A Creative Revolutionary

Belgrano lived in an age of utopias. The son of an Italian man and an Argentine woman of Spanish ancestry, he had devoted himself to the study of law at some of the best universities of the mother country, Spain: Salamanca, Madrid, and Valladolid. In the convulsed Europe of the end of the century, the young Belgrano had not only learned the discipline he had set out to study, but he had become interested in the whirlwind of emerging ideas that had given shape to a new epoch. In particular, political economy. Firmly convinced by the most advanced ideas of progress of his time, he resolutely formed a project within himself: to put all this at the service of the great cause of his native land. Thus, in 1794 he was named the first Perpetual Secretary of the Royal Consulate of Industry and Commerce of the Viceroyalty of Rio de la Plata, something similar to what today would be a finance minister or secretary of commerce. It was not common for strongly centralized Bourbon Spain to place the son of a colonial woman and a foreigner in a post of such importance. But in Buenos Aires men of such formation were scarce. It did not take long for the brand new secretary to confront the American reality when trying to accomplish his task of promoting production and commerce with a really transformative spirit. He quickly realized that the brilliant ideals about the rights of man and of progress collided with the conservative mentality of the colonial administration and the comfortable strata of Buenos Aires, merchants who benefited from the Spanish monopoly and from contraband. He would say in his brief autobiography:

> I knew that nothing would be done in favor of the provinces by some men who subordinated the general interest to their own. Nevertheless, since the obligations of my employment permitted me to talk and

write about such useful subjects, I decided, at least, to sow some seeds that some day might bear fruit, whether because some individuals, propelled by the same spirit, devoted themselves to their cultivation, or whether because the very nature of things made them germinate.

What were these seeds? "To found schools is to cultivate souls", our hero would say. The revolutionary spirit of Belgrano rapidly discovered that the new—that which could become capable of modifying a static and sclerotic reality—would come through education. In this way, he promoted by every means the creation of schools, both for basic education and specialization. *The Consulate Annual Memorials*, the journal *Telégrafo Mercantil*, and later, the *Correo de Comercio*, would be some of the means through which he would seek to *sow those seeds*. His message would insist on the need for technical teaching, designing projects for schools of agriculture, commerce, architecture, mathematics, drafting. Of all these, only those of navigation and drafting were realized. Much before anyone else, Belgrano understood that education and even training in modern disciplines and techniques were an important key for the development of his country. If his projects could not be developed, it was because—as he himself would write years later—"all failed either in the government of Buenos Aires or in the Royal Court in Madrid, or among the business people themselves, individuals who made up this group, for whom there was no other reason or justice or utility or necessity than their mercantile interests; anything that clashed with them encountered a veto, without further recourse." But he did not on this account abandon his effort;

by one means or another he managed to continue disseminating his ideas and putting them into practice. Because in addition to being an idealist, the creator of the flag was supremely persevering, and he did not allow himself to be defeated easily, despite his moderate and conciliating character.

In addition to what he did with economic development, Belgrano considered that "*a cultivated people can never be enslaved.*" The *dignity of the human person* occupied a central position in his mentality, at once Christian and enlightened. From this came his toil also for the foundation of schools in the city and in the countryside, where all children would receive their elementary instruction in literacy, together with a basic training in mathematics, the catechism, and some useful trades to earn their living.

"Those miserable huts where you see multitudes of children, who arrive at puberty without having exercised anything but idleness, must be dealt with to the last detail", he wrote in 1796. "One of the principal means that ought to be adopted toward this end are free schools, where these unfortunates can send their children, without having to pay anything for their instruction; there they could be taught good precepts and be inspired with a love of work, since in a country where idleness reigns, commerce decays and misery takes its place."

No, very different in spirit was his insistence (in the regulations of the School of Geometry, Architecture, Perspective, and Drafting, written in his own hand) upon equal rights for Spaniards, their descendants born in the Viceroyalty, and Indians, and in the provision of four places for orphans, "the most dispossessed of our land". Along the same lines, Belgrano assigns a fundamental importance to the education of girls, in an era which was still very far from practical recognition of equal conditions and rights for men and women. Thus we see a true creator in action, someone who, far from being satisfied with the position he had achieved and exploiting it for his own self-interest, devoted the better part of his energies in trying to sketch the outline of a new society, different, better for everyone. Open to the most advanced ideas of his time and—at the same time –attentive to the necessity that no one be left out of this new world which was taking shape. But something more: it was not a matter of an idealist who avoided the practical difficulties of his projects. He sought to anticipate the means of financing, the material and human resources that would make all of them possible. On this point he did not hesitate himself to make material contributions that would be necessary to sustain a serious educational effort. Shortly after the 1810 Revolution he gave 165 volumes to the public library of Buenos Aires (today the Biblioteca Nacional, the National Library). Likewise, it is known that he dedicated the 40,000 peso prize that he won for his victory in the battle of Salta to the construction of four schools in Tarija, Salta, Tucumán, and Santiago del Estero. He himself wrote up the charter for these schools, in which he laid out how these resources must be used to maintain the teachers, provide tools and books to the children of poor parents, and so forth. A remarkable detail: he held that the teacher should be considered as "Father of the Country" and should hold a seat on the local town council. Another detail, this one not so remarkable: these schools were never built.

"What You See Is Not
Everything That There Is"

Before it starts to look as though the archbishop is trying to transform himself into a history professor, I would like to retrieve some *lessons about creativity* from what we have seen. Beyond the profound differences between the historical periods, there is much that is permanent and valid in the attitude of Belgrano of trying always to look beyond, of not remaining mired in the known, the good or bad of the present. This *utopian* attitude, in the most valuable sense of the word, is undoubtedly one of the essential components of creativity. Paraphrasing (and inverting) a popular expression, we could say that creativity that emerges from hope affirms that "*what you see . . . is not everything that there is.*"

In this way the challenge of being creative requires us to be suspicious of all discourse, thought, affirmation, or proposals that present themselves as "the only possible way". There is always more. There is always another possibility. Perhaps more arduous, perhaps more risky, perhaps more resisted by those who are firmly established and for whom things are going very well. . . . We Argentines have already suffered from that kind of discourse for the past decade, with the entire weight and brilliance of academia and science, with the supreme wisdom of specialists and degrees. Vain promises of the *gurus* of the day, and we have seen where they ended up. Today everybody seems to know *what ought to have been done rather than what was done.* And everybody seems to forget that *what was done* was presented by the *idols* of economic wisdom and the *opinion-shapers* in the field of communication as the only possible path. To be creative, on the contrary, is to affirm *that there is always an open horizon*. And it is not simply a matter of idiotic optimism that we try to copy from a dignitary of two centuries ago.

The affirmation that "what you see is not everything that there is" derives directly from faith in the Risen Christ, the definitive innovation, which declares as provisional and incomplete every other accomplishment, innovation that measures the distance between the present and the manifestation of the new heaven and new earth. A distance that only hope and its active arm achieve: creativity that puts the lie to every false consummation and opens new horizons and alternatives.

What to say, in addition, of the tombstones which we can place over a person—a student, a companion—when we classify, label and bundle him up under a heading, a definition, a *concept*. How many times can we close off paths of renovation and growth of a person or an educational institution, when we resignedly declare that "that's the way things are", "they work that way", or that "with so-and-so you just can't do anything". Of all the possible institutions, it is precisely those animated with Christian faith that ought least to resign themselves and remain with the "already known". *Our schools are called to be real signs, living, that "what you see is not all there is"*, that another world, another country, another society, another school, another family is possible. Called to be institutions where new forms of relationship, new paths of fraternity, a new respect for the unprecedented of each human being, a greater openness and sincerity, a work relationship characterized

by collaboration, where relations of manipulation, competition, *behind-the-back* maneuvers, authoritarianism and
interested favoritisms are left at the door. All closed, definitive discussion always conceals many deceptions; it hides
what must not be seen. It tries to muzzle the truth, which is
always open to the authentically definitive, which is nothing of this world. We think of a school that is open to the
new, capable of surprising itself, and itself open to learning everything and from everyone. A school rooted in the
truth, which is always surprising. A school that is a seed,
in the sense in which Belgrano used the term, and above
all, in the sense of the evangelical word, of a world that is
new, transfigured.

I make you *a proposition*: in a society where lies, cover-
ups and hypocrisy have caused the loss of the basic confidence that makes social bonds possible, what change could
be more revolutionary than *the truth*? To speak with truth;
to tell the truth; to explain our criteria, our values, our
opinions. If at this very moment we forbid ourselves to
pursue any type of lie or dissimulation, we will be also, as
a superabundant effect, more responsible and even more
charitable. The lie dilutes everything, the truth manifests
what there is in the heart. First proposal: *let us always
tell the truth in and from our schools*. I assure you that the
change will be notable: something new will become present
in the midst of our community.

"All of Man, All of Men"

There is a truly evangelical standard that is infallible for
unmasking *lone thoughts* that close off the possibility of

hope, and even false utopias that pervert it. It is the standard of *universality*. *"All of man and all of men"* was the principle of discernment that Paul VI proposed in relation to true development. The preferential option for the poor of the Latin American Episcopate sought nothing else: to include all persons in the totality of their dimensions, in the project of a better society. It would be for this reason that Manuel Belgrano's insistence on an education for all, especially for the most needy, in order to guarantee a full universality, sounds so familiar to us. In reality, can a society that pushes aside a large or small proportion of its members be a desirable one? Even from the egoistic point of view, how can I be sure that I won't be the next one to be excluded?

Perhaps our society has learned something of this in the past year. "There were always poor people among us", but in the last decades the institutions that had attempted to guarantee for all at least the opportunity to live a decent life have been collapsing one by one.

For a long time work, the protection of social insurance, have been disappearing and have been devalued; provincial economies have been breaking apart. . . . Today we are horrified to see that children die of malnutrition. But a few years ago, those of us who were included in the world of consumption neither dreamed (nor wanted to dream) that at the same time that some became citizens of the first world, others were descending into a kind of underworld without work, without meaning, without hope, without a future, decreed to be *non-viable* or only the object of assistance (always insufficient) by an unjust and heartless system. Not until the bank freeze and collapse arrived did many Argentines discover that the infernal machine was also coming for them, for those who had felt safe.

If we accept *yes for some, no for others*, the door is open for all the aberrations that come afterward. And this, also, is a central point of creativity that we are seeking. The capacity always to look at what happens on the side that was not taken into account in the calculations. *To turn back to look*, to see if nobody was left out, nobody forgotten. For many reasons. First, because in the logic of Christianity, *every man must have his place and each is indispensable.* Second, because an exclusive society is, in reality, a society that is the enemy of all. And third, because that which was forgotten will not resign itself so easily. If it was unable to enter through the door, it will try the window. Result: the beautiful exclusive amnesiac society will have to become more and more repressive, to avoid having the Lazaruses who were left outside knocking something off the table of Dives.

Well then, an essential mission of every Christian educator is *to commit entirely to inclusion*, to work for inclusion. Has this not been an ancient practice of the Church, to take education to the most forgotten? Haven't many congregations and educational works been created with this objective? Have we always been consistent with this vocation of service and inclusion? What winds have blown us off course from this evangelical aim? Because the Church also dreams of affording free education for all who desire to receive its service, especially the most poor. But where does this leave us?

It is obvious that things do not fall from the sky like manna, and that in these times it is not easy to maintain our institutions. Of course the state also has its responsibility and its function, and needs in various ways to guarantee free and quality education for all, respecting the freedom of choice which the poor also enjoy. But now I am referring rather to the question of mentality. The mentality with which we proceed with our schools, the mentality with which we transmit, the mentality with which we make decisions and choose options. Our schools must govern themselves according to a well defined standard: *fraternal solidarity*. And this must be the distinctive seal of all and each of its dimensions and activities; and also, allow me to say, that of each one of its Christian teachers. By no means is their work a mere commercial transaction. No work is ever simply that, but yours in particular is not. It is *a service* to persons, to little ones, to persons who place themselves in your hands so that you can help them to become what they can be. "Fathers of the Country", Belgrano called you, and demanded a seat on the Council for you. I wish all our educational institutions could reward our teachers as they ought!

Not just economically: also by respect, participation, recognition. In the economic sphere, reality imposes limits that we cannot deny. But everyone: teachers, directors, pastors, fathers and mothers, students, all of us can be signs of a different world where each is recognized, accepted, included, dignified, and not only for his utility but for his intrinsic value as a human being, son or daughter of God. As we are called to be creative in this critical moment of our country, we will have to ask ourselves what we do as a Church, as a school, as teachers, to contribute a *truly inclusive and universal mentality and practice*, and an education that offers possibilities not to some, but to all who are within our purview, through the variety of means at our disposal.

A *second proposal*: Let us dare to align ourselves wholeheartedly with the Christian value of fraternal solidarity. Let us not allow the individualistic and competitive mentality rooted in our urban culture to end by colonizing our schools as well. Let us rouse ourselves to teach and even to demand generosity, the primacy of the common good. Equality and respect for all: foreigners (from bordering nations), poor, indigent. From our schools, let us combat every form of discrimination and prejudice. Let us learn and teach to give even from the scarce resources of our families and institutions. And let this be manifested in each decision, each word, each project. That way, we will be giving a very clear sign (and even a polemical and controversial one, if necessary) of the different society we wish to create.

"The Road to Hell Is Paved with Good Intentions"

A third guideline to orient our creativity. Once more, we recognize it in the actions of the creator of the national flag, a man who always sought to secure the resources and means to realize his projects. Intentions were not sufficient, nor were words. It is necessary to put our shoulders to the wheel, and do so effectively. It is very nice to talk about solidarity, about a different society, to theorize about school and the importance of an updated, personalized education, with our feet firmly on the ground. There are tons of words about the information society, about knowledge as the first principle of the world at present, et cetera, et cetera. But *"the road to hell is paved with good intentions."* A true creativity, as we have already seen, does not neglect the ends, the values, the meaning. But neither does it set aside the concrete aspects of project implementation. *Technique* without *ethics* is empty and dehumanizing —a blind man guiding other blind men—but a proposal of ends without *an adequate consideration of the means* to attain it is condemned to become a mere fantasy. Utopia, we said, in the same way as it has this capacity to mobilize by situating itself *before* and *outside* of the limited and problematic, also, and for this very reason, has an aspect of madness, of alienation, in the measure that it does not develop interventions in order to make the objectives of its attractive visions possible.

For this reason, in order to confront the present moment creatively, we must continually develop our capacities, polish our tools, deepen our knowledge. Reconstructing our feeble educational system, from the limited or prominent place that we occupy, implies training, responsibility, professionalism. Nothing is done without the necessary resources, not only the economic but also human talents. Creativity is not for the mediocre. But nor is it for *luminaries* or *geniuses*: although there is always a need for dreamers and prophets, their word falls into the void without builders who know their trade.

The school that is placed on the front lines to respond to these challenges must enter into a dynamic of dialogue and participation in order to resolve the new problems in new ways, knowing that no one has a monopoly on knowledge or inspiration, and that the responsible and competent contribution of each is critical. Socioeconomic

exclusion, the crisis of meaning and values, and the desta-
bilizing of the social bond are a reality that touches everyone, but in a special way it affects our children and adolescents. It has become necessary to look for effective means
of accompanying them and strengthening them in the face
of the risks that press in upon them. And not only AIDS
or drugs; also individualism, frustrating consumerism, the
lack of opportunities, temptation to violence and despair,
the loss of connections and horizons, the limitation of the
ability to love. Are we prepared? Can we count on adequate
teams of professionals? Are we setting out to look for experiences, knowledge, proposals, or do we tend to stick to
what we know, whether it works or not? Are we ready to
set up networks, with a generous opening to the diocesan
dimension? If we add *a prudential and generous administration of our human and institutional talent* to a true Christian mysticism of opening to the future and to universal
and concrete solidarity, not contenting ourselves with what
we already have but seeking to perfect our skills and abilities ever more, we will be in a condition to respond to the
present moment with an authentically creative attitude.

And here is the *third proposal: let us not hesitate to look
for the best in our schools.* Let us shake free of a certain
short-sightedness, a tendency to want to "patch it up with
baling wire" that has been the habit of our communities
for a long time. Let us be concerned that our teachers, our
chaplains, our administrators, be really good and serious
in their respective domains. Spirit is important, but also
professional competence. Not in order to fall into the myth
of *excellence* in the competitive or nonsupportive sense in
which it sometimes presents itself, but rather to offer our

community and our nation the best of ourselves, investing fully of our talents.

Creativity and Tradition: "To Build from Strength"

Creativity, which is nourished by utopia, is rooted in solidarity and seeks the most effective means, can still suffer from a pathology that perverts it to the point of converting it into the worst of ills: the belief that everything begins with us, a defect that, as we already noted, degenerates rapidly into authoritarianism. Let us return to 1810. A few months after the May Revolution, Belgrano is sent on a military mission to Paraguay. One year later, he will be placed in charge of the Army of the North with the mission of combating important royalist enclaves in the North. With victories and reverses, he will occupy this post until 1814, at which time he is replaced by San Martín. Obviously, we are not going to embark on the chronicle of the military campaigns of the lawyer placed in command of armies, but I would like to call attention to a detail which shows us the attitude of the hero and which can give us a foothold to develop our last reflection about creativity. You will know that Belgrano was a leader who was truly recognized and loved by his subordinates, but that also, throughout the troops, there circulated certain commentaries of a facetious and mocking character: that he was strait-laced, that he had a weak character. . . . It is true that, for those soldiers, the son of comfortable merchants, trained in the best centers of Buenos Aires and of Spain, always devoted to books and intellectual endeavors, would undoubtedly have a rather distant aspect. But it is also true that a great part of these criticisms were related to his moderate attitude and, above all, to his strict prohibitions with regard to dealings with women, alcohol, fighting, gambling, and other issues dealing with military discipline. It is that Belgrano considered that military campaigns undertaken in the name of the Revolution had to be at the height of the ideals that animated these revolutionary campaigns, ideals of the dignity of man, of liberty and fraternity, all in addition founded in the Christian virtues. For this reason, he required of his troops a true testimony of *integrity* and of *respect* for the communities through which they passed.

He was especially severe with everything that could bring scandal to the religious beliefs of the villages of the interior. In a proclamation to the troops upon their entrance into Alto Peru [present-day Bolivia], he ordered: "the usages, customs, and even the concerns of the villages will be respected; anyone who mocks them with actions, words, or even gestures will be executed."

In addition to his own religious convictions, for him *the meaning of the Revolution was in play*, and in the final analysis, *that of the nation that he wished to build*. Indeed, in one of his letters to San Martín, who was already at the head of the Northern Army, Belgrano wrote, "[Y]ou must wage the war [in Alto Peru] not only with arms, but with public opinion, holding firm to the natural Christian and religious virtues, since the enemy has stained our reputation, calling us heretics, and only by this means have they attracted barbarous people to arms, claiming that we were attacking religion. (. . .) One must not allow oneself to be carried away by extravagant opinions, nor by men who do not know the country that they traverse." It was not irrelevant to these precautions that military and civilian leaders had seriously scandalized the inhabitants of those places in the past with their anti-Catholic attitudes and exhortations, typical of the enlightenment mentality of the French Revolution. On the contrary, Belgrano knew that *nothing can be built on the indiscriminate destruction of what went before, but that it must start from the recognition of the identity and the value of the other.*

And here is where we conclude our overview concerning creativity as located within the *tension between change and continuity.* If being creative has to do with being capable of opening oneself to the new, this does not mean neglecting the element of continuity with the past. Only God creates out of nothing, we said earlier. And thus as there is no way of healing the sick if we do not rely upon what is healthy in him, in the same way *we cannot create something new in history if it is not based on the materials which history itself affords us.*

Belgrano recognized that the united and strong America of which he dreamed could only be built on respect and the affirmation of the identity of the people. If creativity is not capable of assuming active aspects of the real and the present, it rapidly becomes an authoritarian imposition, the brutal replacement of one truth by another. Might this not be one of the keys to our difficulty in moving ahead with a more positive dynamic? If in building we always tend to overturn and trample what others have done before, how can we found something solid? How can we avoid sowing new hatreds that later on will bring to nought what we have been trying to do?

For this reason, if as educators we want truly to sow the seeds of a more just, free, and fraternal society, we need to learn to *recognize the historical successes* of our founders, of our artists, thinkers, politicians, educators, pastors. . . . Perhaps now we are realizing that in the season of the *fat cows* we had allowed ourselves to be dazzled by *rose-colored glasses*, intellectual and other fashions, and we had forgotten some of the certainties learned very painfully by earlier generations: the value of social justice, hospitality, solidarity among the generations, work as the dignification of the person, the family as the basis of society. . . .

Our schools ought to be a space where our children and youth can *make contact with the vitality of our history.* Not just in costumes of picturesque sellers of the typical maize and milk dessert, the "mazamorra", often seen during the festivities of the twenty-fifth of May celebrating the revolution that led to our independence, but also learning to reflect on the good decisions and the errors that constitute our present reality. But this assumes that before, all of us, as educators, have been able to accomplish this process—together. Beyond the various options and forms of thinking, it is necessary to learn to elaborate basic shared agreements—that do not sink to the lowest common denominator—on which to be able to continue building. It is the only way of affirming a collective identity in which everyone can recognize himself.

Creating from what exists also assumes being able to *recognize the differences, the knowledge* and even the limits of our children and their families. We know that education is in no way a one-directional process. But do we act according to this knowledge? Are we really ready to allow ourselves to be taught, ourselves, the teachers? Are we able to take on the responsibility of a relationship from which we can all emerge changed? Do we believe in our pupils, in the families of our neighborhood, in our people? The capacity to "build from strength" is, then, the fourth and last standard for creative action that I want to share with you today.

And I make the *final proposal*: let us rouse ourselves to *propose models of life* to our pupils. The postmodern culture, which dilutes everything, has declared every proposal of concrete ethics to be out of date. To present valuable examples of service, of struggle for justice, of compromise for the sake of the community, of sanctity and heroism, tends to be seen as a kind of useless or pernicious *time tunnel*. And over a devastated territory, what remains but the survival instinct? Paraphrasing a song which you undoubtedly know and have sung, "Who said that everything is lost? Many have offered their heart." Let us testify with the conviction that these offerings have not been in vain. And before the steamroller of "everything is equal, nothing is better", we will have placed undeniable signs that something new is possible.

Conclusion

Our reflection has left us with *four teachings* about historical creativity that it is necessary to engage at this time, four *principles of discernment*:

- Always to look beyond: "What you see is not all that there is."

- Always to take account of "every man and all men".
- Always to look for the most appropriate and effective means: "The road to hell is paved with good intentions."
- To "build from strength", salvaging the positive values and achievements.

And, as a way (and not the only one) of putting into practice the foregoing, four proposals:

- Always tell the truth.
- Risk everything for the sake of fraternal solidarity.
- Continually develop our abilities.
- Bear witness and propose concrete models for life.

Like the miracle of Jesus, our bread and fishes can be multiplied (Mt 14:17–20). As in the example given by our Lord to his disciples, our little offering has a maximum value (Lk 21:1–4). As in the parable, our little seeds become a tree and a harvest (Mt 13:23, 31–32). All of this from the living fountain of the Eucharist, in which our bread and our wine are transfigured in order to give us life eternal. An immense and difficult task is given to us. In faith in the Resurrected One, we can confront it with creativity and hope, and placing ourselves always in the position of the servants in that wedding, astonished collaborators in the first sign of Jesus, who merely followed the instructions of a woman: "Do whatever he tells you" (Jn 2:5). Creativity and hope make *life* increase. This year, synthesizing all of this, we want to say most forcefully: to educate is to choose life, let us ask it of our Mother with the words of John Paul II in *Evangelium Vitae*:

O Mary,
bright dawn of the new world,
Mother of the living,
to you do we entrust the cause of life:
Look, O Mother,
upon the vast numbers
of babies not allowed to be born,
of the poor whose lives are made difficult,
of men and women
who are victims of inhuman violence,
of the elderly and the sick killed
by indifference or out of misguided mercy.
Grant that all who believe in your Son
may proclaim the Gospel of life
with firmness and love
to the people of our time.
Obtain for them the grace
to embrace that Gospel
as a gift ever new,
the happiness of celebrating it with gratitude
throughout their lives
and the courage to bear witness to it resolutely,
    in order to build,
together with all people of good will,
the civilization of truth and love,
to the praise and glory of God,
the Creator and lover of life.
Amen.

—Buenos Aires, during Lent
of the year of our Lord 2003

Key to Reading
for Working Individually or in Groups

✐ Let's reflect

If we say that utopia, "far from being a mere consoling fantasy, an imaginary estrangement, is a form taken by hope in a concrete historical situation":

FOR PERSONAL REFLECTION

—What are the foundations of my hope?

—In what moments of my life have I experienced the need for hope?

—In whom have I found a model in order to live in hope?

FOR WORK IN GROUPS

—What is the evolution of our society during the past ten years according to the following parameters: confidence, tolerance and solidarity?

—What are the characteristics of utopia that encourage our hope?

—What positive elements do we find in our society that we may build upon?

🖜 **Let's read**

"You know what hour it is, how it is full time now for you to wake from sleep. For salvation is nearer to us now than when we first believed; the night is far gone, the day is at hand. Let us then cast off the works of darkness and put on the armor of light."

                                                           —*Romans 13:11–12*

🖜 **Let's think**

"The Church fulfills her obligation to foster in her children a full awareness of their rebirth to a new life. It is precisely in the Gospel of Christ, taking root in the minds and lives of the faithful, that the Catholic school finds its definition as it comes to terms with the cultural conditions of the times."

                                                           —*The Catholic School, 9*

🖜 **Let's review our task**

Msgr. Bergoglio leaves us four clear lines to orient our activity as educators. Let us review the text.

1. "To be creative, on the contrary, is to affirm *that there is always an open horizon*. And it is not simply a matter of idiotic optimism that we try to copy from a dignitary of two centuries ago. The affirmation that 'what you see is not everything that there is' derives directly from faith in the Risen Christ, the definitive innovation, which declares as provisional and incomplete every other accomplishment,

innovation that measures the distance between the present
and the manifestation of the new heaven and new earth. A
distance that *only hope and its active arm achieve: creativity*
that puts the lie to every false consummation and opens
new horizons and alternatives."

—How do we confront the temptation of resigning ourselves to the impossibility of renovating our educational
institutions?

—What signs of stagnation do we detect in our standards?

—What are the circumstances in which, as an educational
institution, we have displayed our creativity?

2. "Now, an indispensable mission of every Christian educator is *to commit entirely to inclusion, to work for inclusion.* Has this not been an ancient practice of the Church,
to take education to the most forgotten? (. . .) Our schools
must govern themselves according to a well defined standard: *fraternal solidarity.* And this must be the distinctive
seal of all and each of its dimensions and activities; and
also, allow me to say, that of each one of its Christian
teachers."

—Have we always been consistent with this vocation of
service and inclusion in our institutions?

—How do we demonstrate this spirit of inclusion in our
educational communities?

—What is the reigning mentality regarding *fraternal solidarity* in the following levels of relationship:

- Among educational institutions
- Among the teachers
- Among the students
- Among the teachers and the students?

3. "The school that is placed on the front lines to respond to these challenges must enter into a dynamic of dialogue and participation in order *to resolve the new problems in new ways*, knowing that no one has a monopoly on knowledge or inspiration, and that the responsible and competent contribution of each is critical. (. . .) Let us shake off a certain shortsightedness, a certain 'fix it up with duct tape' style which has been a long-time habit of our communities. Let us take care that our teachers, our directors, our administrators, *be really good and serious in their posts.*"

—What are the new problems in our institution that we must confront?

—What shall we do to avoid stagnation in our human and professional development?

—Do we go out in search of experiences, knowledge and suggestions, or do we tend to stick with what we already know, whether it works or not?

4. "If being creative has to do with being capable of opening oneself to the new, this does not mean neglecting the element of continuity with the past. Only God creates out of nothing, we said earlier. (. . .) If creativity is not capable of assuming active aspects of the real and the present, it rapidly becomes an authoritarian imposition, the brutal

replacement of one *truth* by another. (. . .) If in building we always tend to overturn and trample what others have done before, how can we found something solid? How can we avoid sowing new hatreds which later on will bring to nought what we have been trying to do?"

—Are we ourselves, the teachers, really prepared to allow ourselves to be taught?

—Are we capable of assuming a relation in which we can all come out changed?

—How can we cultivate the capacity to *build from strength*?

✍ **Let us pray**

> Lord,
> Grant that I may strive not so much
> to be called a good teacher but to be a
> good teacher; not so much to speak of
> Thee, but to reveal Thee; not so
> much to talk about Thee; not so much
> to speak about love and human
> service, but to be the spirit of
> these; not so much to speak of the
> ideals of Jesus, but in every act of
> my teaching to reveal his ideals.
>
> *—Wallace Grant Fisk*

2

With Courage, among Us All, a Country that Educates

Jesus, Incarnate Wisdom of God

Dear educators: There's nothing new about saying that we live in difficult times. You know it, you feel it tangibly day by day in the classroom. You surely have felt many times that your strength is not up to dealing with the anguish that burdens your families and their expectations of you. This is the focus of this year's message, which invites you to discover once again the greatness of the vocation that you have received. If we look at *Jesus, incarnate Wisdom of God*, we will be able to realize that difficulties become challenges, challenges call forth hope and generate happiness in knowing yourselves to be the architects of something new. All this surely impels us to continue giving the best of ourselves.

These are the things that I want to share with you today. We Christians have a specific contribution to make to our country, and you, educators, must be the protagonists of a change that is urgent. I invite you to this and place my confidence in you for this, and I offer you my service as [your] pastor.

In this past year it became popular to say that *we Argentines have "recovered hope"*. It remains to be seen if it is a matter of that authentic hope that opens a qualitatively different future (although it may not have an explicitly religious designation), or if we are disposed simply to go back to deluding ourselves once more. In any case, we are going to take this *change of mood* as a point of departure for the purpose of making some reflections. Sticking to what concerns us here, which is the question of the values that sustain and justify our task as educators, I propose to situate us in a scenario that can give rise to interesting considerations: *the scenario of the reconstruction of community*.

The panorama of recent years in our country has led us to recognize a *fundamental* problem, a crisis of beliefs and values and, like every recognition, places before us the challenge of looking for a solution. Here is where the idea of *reconstruction* turns out to be rather more than a metaphor. It is not a question of *turning back* as if nothing had been learned. Neither is it a question of *getting rid* of something pernicious, a kind of tumor of our collective conscience, supposing that previously the organism possessed *complete health*. If we speak of *reconstruction* it is because we are conscious of the impossibility of leapfrogging and bypassing the historical. *To reconstruct* means in this case *once again to put in the forefront ends, desires, and ideals, and to find new and more effective ways of orienting our actions* toward these ends, desires, and ideals, articulating efforts and generalizing realities (exterior and interior, institutions and habits) which permit the coherent and shared participation in the march forward.

No one is unaware that education is one of the principal pillars for this reconstruction of the sense of community, although it cannot be dissociated from other equally fundamental dimensions like the economic and the political. The diagnosis locates the crisis not only in the errors of a macroeconomy that is lacking in vision (or a vision that is distorted in its place and function in a national community) but also at a political, cultural and—yet more deeply —moral level; if this diagnosis is accurate, the task will be long and will consist more in a *sowing* than in a series of rapid modifications. For this reason, I do not think I am exaggerating if I affirm that *any project that does not put education in a priority position will simply be "more of the same"*.

Now then, as Christian educators facing the challenge of making our contribution to the reconstruction of the national community, we need to perform a series of *discernments* concerning what, at least in our judgment, should be prioritized. The fruitfulness of our efforts depends not only on the subjective conditions, the degree of dedication, generosity and commitment we can attain, it also depends on the *"objective" correctness* of our decisions and actions.

To understand, interpret, and discern are indispensable moments of all responsible and consistent action, of every path of hope. As Christians we have a point of departure, a reference that offers itself as a light and guide. We do not walk blindly, feeling our way in the search for meaning by orienting ourselves simply by a process of *trial and error*.

Christian discernment is Christian precisely because it takes as its central point *Jesus Christ, the Wisdom of God* (1 Cor 1:24-30). If it is a matter of *understanding*, of *giving meaning*, of *knowing* where we are going, we Christians have an inexhaustible source which is the divine Wisdom made flesh, made man, made history. There we must return, over and over, in search of illumination, inspiration and strength.

Our Foundation:
Christ, the Wisdom of God

The Three Aspects of Wisdom

What does it mean to speak about wisdom? In the first place, it is clear that it is a matter of *something in the order of knowledge*. It is the first meaning of *to know*: to be acquainted with, to understand. To be wise, to live with wisdom, implies many things but the *intellectual* aspect can never be set aside. As educators, service to the wisdom of our people is—in large measure—a service to growth in the cognitive order. If today we have in mind the existential, affective, relational, attitudinal aspects . . . all of this cannot be at the expense of a strong stake in the intellectual. In this we must recognize that there is an aspect of truth at the very origins—perhaps rooted in the Enlightenment or the encyclopedia—and at the *foundation* of Argentine education. A person who knows more, who has cultivated his capacity to inform himself, evaluate and reflect, to incorporate new ideas and place them in relation to previous ideas in order to produce new meanings, has in his hands an invaluable tool not merely to open up a path in the arena of work and *success* in social life; he also possesses elements that are extremely valuable for developing as a person, to grow in the sense of *being* better.

It is not in vain that the Church has always seen the importance of intellectual activity as well as the strictly religious in education. Knowledge is not only "portable", as our grandmothers used to tell us, but it *opens up space, multiplies places* for human development.

Here, still at the beginning of our meditation, we already have a concrete point from which to review and converse in our educational communities. Very rightly we put the accent on community life, on amplifying our capacity for welcoming and stability, in creating human ties and environments of happiness and love, which permit our children and young people to grow and bear fruit. And we do well in so doing: many times these basic contributions are denied them by a society that is ever harder, success-driven, competitive, individualistic. But all that *cannot be done at the cost of the essential task of feeding and forming the intelligence.* These days the word *excellence* is fashionable, sometimes with an ambiguous meaning which we will re turn to, but let us rescue from this fad *the imperative of working seriously on the plane of the transmission and creation of knowledge of all kinds.* Paraphrasing this fashionable term: *let us seek an education "of the intelligence".*

But wisdom is not exhausted by knowledge. To know— *saber*—in Spanish also means *to taste.* Knowledge is known —*saber*—and flavors are tasted—*saber.* What does this dimension add to what we have been saying? The *"affective" aspect and the "aesthetic":* we know and we love what we taste. To educate, then, will be much more than offering knowledge: it will be to help our children and young people to evaluate and contemplate it, to make it flesh. It presupposes a work not only of the intelligence but also of the will. We posit personal freedom as the ultimate synthesis of the human mode of being in the world, but not an indeterminate liberty (nonexistent!) but rather fertilized

by experiences of security, of joy, of love given and received. I am not talking about children "liking" to go to
school to learn. The search for wisdom as *savoring* is not
reduced to a question of *motivation*, although it includes
it. It is a matter of their being able to *feel* the joy of words,
of giving and receiving, of listening and sharing, of understanding the world which surrounds them and the ties
that unite them to it, to marvel at the mystery of creation and its culminating point: man. We will return to
these questions. For now, let us take note that our educational task has to *awaken the sentiment of the world and
society as home. To educate "to be at home"*: indispensable
path to being human and recognizing ourselves as children
of God.

I still want to call your attention to a third *aspect*, a third
dimension of wisdom. Wise is he who not only knows about
things, contemplates them and loves them, but who suc-
ceeds in integrating himself with them through the *choice of
a direction* and the *multiple concrete and even daily options*
that fidelity requires. A *"practical"* aspect, then, in which
the two previous ones are resolved. This dimension coin-
cides with the former meaning present in the Bible: the capacity to orient oneself in life, in order that a prudent and
skillful work bears fruit in existential fullness and happiness. *To know* what is "worthwhile" and what is not:
an *ethical wisdom* that, far from constraining and inhibit-
ing human possibilities, unfolds and develops them to their
maximum. A moral knowledge opposed equally to *immoral*
as to *demoralized*. Also to know *"how to do it"*: a practical knowledge, *not only relative to ends but with available
means in order not to be stuck in good intentions*. This third
dimension of wisdom is that which King Solomon asked

for as a grace to be able to govern his people (cf. Wis 9:1–11).

We want a school of wisdom . . . like a kind of existential, ethical, and social laboratory, where children and young people can experience whatever things permit them to develop in fullness and construct the skills necessary to carry forward their life projects. A place where *wise* teachers, that is to say, persons whose routine and whose impact personify a model of a *desirable* life, offer elements and resources that, for those who are beginning their journey, can save them something of the suffering of having to do it *from scratch*, experiencing wrong or destructive choices in their own flesh.

To promote a wisdom that implies knowledge, evaluation, and practice is an ideal worthy to preside over any educational undertaking. Whoever can contribute something in this way to his community will have contributed to the collective happiness in an incalculable degree. And, as we said, we Christians possess in Jesus Christ a principle of fullness of wisdom that we do not have the right to restrict within our confessional space. The evangelization which our Lord urges refers to nothing else: *to share a wisdom that from the beginning was destined for all men and women of all times.* Let us renew audaciously the ardor of the announcement, of the offer that we know envelops deep searches, silenced by so much confusion, let us do it daily and try to reach everyone.

To Build on Rock

This is our conviction as Christians. But we still have to undertake much discernment in order to understand the *radical newness* of which we are custodians. When all is said and done, the historical failures and even the most incredible horrors and aberrations we have lived through in our country have sometimes had as protagonists our own brothers who confessed the same faith and shared our observances. *To proclaim the name of Jesus Christ does not exempt either error or evil.* Jesus himself has already said it: it is not enough to say, "Lord, Lord!" if one does not do the will of the Father (Mt 7:21–23). It is not just a matter of *bad intention*, or of "wolves in sheep's clothing". It is very easy to say that "when all is said and done, at the bottom of their heart, they were never one of us": thus we preserve our merely nominal security, expelling those elements that would make us question ourselves on the depth and solidity of our beliefs and practices.

Let us continue paying attention to the words of the Lord we have just recalled. In the verses that follow, Jesus pursues his teaching with the parable of the man who builds his house on a rock. "The rain fell, and the floods came, and the winds blew and beat upon that house, but it did not fall, because it had been founded on the rock" (Mt 7:25). The images of *rain*, *floods*, and *winds* can give a certain impression of passivity to this construction: simply *endure*. *Endure*, maintaining one's faith, one's convictions, in the middle of the world's adversities. But the immediate relation of the parable with the earlier declarations of Jesus (it is not enough to say "Lord, Lord . . .") situates us in a completely different place; they refer to more. It is a question of doing *"the will of my Father* who is in heaven" (Mt 7:21), or *to do what Jesus, the master, tells us* (Lk 6:46). It is a matter of *resisting the battering of the world*, and even more, *"putting one's shoulder to the wheel"* in a task that is closely connected to the Kingdom which is revealed in Jesus.

What then does it mean "to build on the rock" to be able to put into practice the will of the Lord? I believe that the idea of *wisdom* permits us to begin opening a way in our search. If the task, the concrete task that we have at hand, the educational task in the context of reconstructing the community, requires a solid subjective compromise and also a serious and lucid objective discernment, then it will have to be overseen by an intellectual, affective, practical Wisdom that puts fully in play the model of Jesus in these three planes. To confess Christ as the Lord, to be apostles in the diffusion of the gospel and in the inauguration of his Kingdom, necessarily implies constructing the building of our Christian and teaching identity, and of our educational action, on the rock of the incarnate Wisdom.

At this point, at which doubtless all of us have arrived in responding to our vocation, we can run across some *misunderstandings* that give rise to true *temptations*.

The first is that of remaining with a purely pious conception of the incarnate Wisdom of Jesus of Nazareth. To make only an *interior, subjective experience* of it, passing over its *objective* side, the real gaze on the world, the movement of the heart toward the light of this understanding, the concrete determination that includes the creation of effective interventions in order to approach the ideal. This is the permanent temptation of the *pseudomystical* tendencies of the Christian existence.

This perspective, while constituting one of the aspects of the Christian mystery (and of all religious mystery), ends by reducing itself to a kind of *elitism of the spirit*, an ecstatic experience of the elect who break with real and concrete history. The enlightened *elites* through an inward dynamic deprive us of the sense of belonging to a people, in this case the people of God which is now the Church. The enlightened elites block every horizon that invites us to continue on, and invert our action inward, in an immanentism without hope. At the bottom of this spiritual elitism, which undermines all wisdom, is the negation of the fundamental truth of our faith: the Word came in the flesh (1 Jn 4:2).

In the New Testament we have a concrete example of this reductionist emphasis: the first Christian community of Corinth, which provoked an energetic letter from Saint Peter. These Christians of Greek origin had developed a conception of the faith of a *charismatic* type, but dissociating the experiences "in the Spirit" (gift of tongues, ecstasies . . .) from their correlated moral and social commitments. Saint Peter had to call their attention to this kind of *spiritual Christianity* that lost connection with daily life at the practical level. It is a matter of a conception more likely to develop what today we call a new age religiosity than an authentic faith in Jesus of Nazareth and his good news. In times like ours of destitution and loss of meaning, this unilaterality of the *mystical* constitutes an experience that undoubtedly is consoling and beneficial. But it is certain that after a certain point, the mystery of the *sinful condition of man* refutes the pretensions to "elevation above the mundane" which this deficient spirituality implies, and forces it to reveal its hidden facet of lying and self-deception.

How would a similar emphasis on Christian wisdom affect our task in the classroom? Among other ways, through a *magical conception of faith and at times of the sacraments.*

I do not intend at this point to analyze the sacramental life of our educational communities. I mention some situations that occur, among others: routine and absence.

Sometimes we turn the signs of the meeting with God into absolutes, to the point of neglecting what they ought to signify; we do nothing but invalidate them, make them lose consistency, render them mechanical. Along the same lines, we have sometimes trusted too much in the *exaltation of the emotional* in catechetical conclaves, in youth retreats, in the good moments experienced in the Day of the Family . . . moments of gratitude, yes, of celebration and happiness, but at times inconsistent. . . . Praise and enjoyment in the Lord are not *instruments* or means for anything but rather express the radiance of a truly evangelical life, and reside on an effectively traveled path, the anticipation of the hoped-for happiness.

Finally, one other way of resembling the Corinthians of Saint Peter: *the cult of spontaneity* . . . translated as *improvisation*. The valid criticism of bureaucratic, mindless formality, of hewing to procedure and regulation, the priority of the *spirit* above the *letter*, can also lead us to mediocrity and ineffectiveness, when it does not lead to the sheer cult of personality, and in conclusion, to the desertion of the mission which has been entrusted to us, making it shipwreck in a lamentable parody of living and creative community that, like lying, is always exposed in the end.

At the other extreme, Christian wisdom becomes *a predominantly "objective" fact*, a *"flag"* above the icon of the historical Christ who did not remain in the grave but was exalted as Lord, that outlines a *new, observable social and*

cultural order, a series of certainties identified with some
concrete historical fulfillment. The *objectivity* of the Resurrection of Christ, according to this reductionist conception, would lead to the *objectivity* of his triumph in history, in the form of an identification between the Kingdom
of God and of this world, which over and over recurs in
the history of the Church and that, already at the dawn
of Christianity, deserved an important critical page of the
Gospel of John in the dialogue between Jesus and Pilate
(Jn 18:33–37). Indeed, why would Jesus reject summoning
his angels to defend his Kingdom? Because this Kingdom
"was not of this world", it was not a matter of some other
political, social, or cultural alternative fatally attached to
the expiration of all that is born, grows, and dies in time.

And if *mystical* Christianity gave rise to a type of elitism
or of "narcissistic celebration", its opposite, the historical extreme, opens the doors to an *"authoritarianism of the
spirit"* which, like the former, ends up inevitably touch-
ing the *flesh* of human beings. Because the *historical condition as a conflict of subjectivities*, as the ambiguous field
where things are never absolutely black or white (cf. the
parable of the wheat and the tares) always brings *perfect
and definitive* orders to grief and forces them to reveal the
capacity of evil that is typical of them. Finally, the will to
dominate which man carries within him emerges, in this
case camouflaged by the contemplation of the triumph of
Christ over death.

This can also affect (and seriously distort) our service
in the educational task. It is clear (although dissenters are
never lacking) that a model of rigid historical identities,
lacking space for dissent and even for diverse and plural-

istic options and orientations, cannot take place now, at least in our Western societies. The place of *subjectivity* in modern culture, recognizing detours and nonsense, is now a conquest of mankind. The evangelical inspiration is not totally disconnected from this development of the concept of the human person as the subject of an inviolable liberty. In the religious plane itself, human dignity requires a type of design and adherence to beliefs that is very far from an imposition of the undisputed immanent letter that chains or diminishes the personal search for God, one that calls forth the rich resources that man received to embark on such a venture.

By no means should our schools aspire to form a hegemonic army of Christians who will know all the answers, but rather they should be the place where all the questions arc welcomed, where, in the light of the gospel, the personal search is encouraged and is not blocked by verbal walls, walls that are pretty weak and that inevitably fall shortly thereafter. The challenge is greater: it demands depth, it demands attention to life, it demands healing and liberating from idols . . . and here we state with precision: the *mystical* as well as the *historical-political* conception configure a triumphalism, a true caricature of the real triumph of Christ over sin and death.

Dimensions of Christian Wisdom

But then, how can we advance in a positive understanding of Christian wisdom? We know that it is not possible here to take more than an initial look, necessarily brief and limited. Nobody can claim to exhaust the infinite richness of the Word made flesh in a simple collection of human words. It is rather a matter of inviting you to search, to pray, to delve into Scripture and the many expressions of the Magisterium and the living tradition of the Church, trying to uncover the accents and heights proper to the faith which becomes life for today's world. I want to exhort you to *a more attentive and vigilant gaze on the signs of the times, to a renewed strengthening of prayer and community reflection*, to recreate that *dialogue of salvation* that, in various moments of history, has brought forth the fruit of sanctity and opened unanticipated instances of evangelization and renewal. This requires of us to make time for commonality, to open ourselves with seriousness and enthusiasm to building together with others, putting our whole heart into the enterprise.

In this way, allow me to share as pastor some ideas that can be valuable to keep in mind. Simply, some aspects in which the person and the word of Jesus give form to the ideal of wisdom sketched out above.

In the first place, *Christian wisdom as truth*. Jesus, he himself, defines himself in this way (Jn 14:6). We have to advance toward an idea of truth ever more inclusive, less restrictive. At least, if we are thinking about the truth of God and not about some human truth, however solid it appears. The truth of God is inexhaustible, it is an ocean from which we barely see the shore. It is something that we are beginning to discover in these times: not to enslave ourselves to an almost paranoid defense of *our truth* (if I *have* it, he doesn't *have* it; if he *can have it*, then I *don't have it*). *The truth is a gift that remains large*, and precisely for this reason it *enlarges us, it amplifies us, it elevates us*. And it makes us servants of such a gift, which does not entail relativisms, but rather that the truth requires a continual path of deepening comprehension.

The gospel of Jesus offers us truth: about God, about a God who is Father, about a God who comes to an encounter with his own, about a free and liberating God who chooses, calls and sends. Let us reread the parables and comparisons to the Kingdom: they speak of God. God wanders the roads because he prepared a feast and wants everyone to enjoy it; God is hidden in the small and in that which grows, although we are unable to see it. God is infinitely generous, he waits to the last moment and goes in search of those who have lost their way. He overpays the last-minute laborers and also does not hold back his love from those of the first hour and from the brother of the prodigal son: on the contrary, he always has them close to him and invites them to transcend themselves and resemble him.

God . . . what can we say, that is not surpassed by the infinity of what he is! When we return to drink from the well of the gospel, we instantly realize how pathetic have been the *representations* of God that men have manufactured throughout history, many times in their own image. But still more: we are talking about *a God who did not remain settled in his "divinity"*. Everything we can say of him has had and has a human mode of existence: that of Jesus of Nazareth. This infinitely merciful and saving Father is not an unreachable figure: He realized his work in the actions and words of the Master.

So, *Christian wisdom is also truth over men.* Over the God-Man, and over the man who is called to live the divine condition. This is an ever new and ever present message:

even in times of technological globalization, where everything human seems to reduce itself to *bits* and it would appear that it has been decided to leave many out of the *kingdom* which is being organized, there is a word of wisdom that repeats itself over and over, in the ear and to the four winds, from pulpit and forums, and also from the Golgothas and many hells of this world, about the unmovable fidelity of a God who wanted to be man so that men could be like God. And achieve this precisely by the opposite path suggested by the serpent in Eden.

I wonder if those of us who have the mission of teaching today can succeed in weighing all the beauty and explosivity of this truth about God and man which we have received. It is now more than a century ago (this year marks 110 years since his death), a Christian realized his vocation as teacher, journalist, and politician from his convictions, fully assuming his condition as a believer and as a man of his time, without dualisms or reservations. I refer to *José Manuel Estrada*, and I believe that it is important to rescue his person not only from the concrete battles in which his faithfulness to the Church and his love of his country were mobilized, but from the selfsame fact that *he understood the Christian truth as an immense power for elevating mankind* and he did not settle for less: for him, it was not a matter of *enduring* the wind and the rain but rather strengthening his abilities for the service of building a new society.

Fully of his time, he shared in the questioning about the meaning of human life and he accurately identified the point where this meaning becomes a question mark and an invitation to the search for all men of good will:

> The comparative sciences, whether they belong to the material order like chemistry or the moral order like

philosophy, classify facts, define phenomena, formulate perhaps their immediate and secondary laws; but
they are impotent to describe the superior connection
that binds them, within their metaphysical conditions
of production, to a universal harmony, subjected to a
sublime law. (. . .) If the ignorance of man consisted
only in impotence in appreciating phenomena and their
conditions, naturalism would suffice to dissipate it
gradually. But this other curiosity, even when the other
curiosities of the visible world and that hidden from
the circumstantial "why" of all experimental facts are
exhausted, will never disappear either from the mind
of the Christian, nor from that of the logical atheist,
nor from the spirit of anyone who raises himself an
iota above the level in which pure animality and bar-
barity mix almost indissolubly: Who am I? Nor this
other: Where do I come from? Nor, finally, this ago-
nizing problem central to the sweetness of faith and
the angst of incredulity or doubt: Where am I going?

But Estrada testifies that Christian wisdom does not remain on the plane of discourse. *The dimension of truth
goes hand in hand with that of life and way.* The "three
aspects" of wisdom reach their evangelical resolution in
Jesus and also in those who followed in his footsteps.
The truth about God and about man is the principle of
*another way of assessing the world, one's fellow man, one's
own life, one's personal mission*; it is the principle of another love. And, necessarily, it is the principle of *ethical
orientations and historical options* that give form to a concrete incarnation of Wisdom in the time in which we happen to live. I invite us to move forward, reflecting on some
ways in which Christian wisdom could model our teaching

vocation, translating the revealed truth in deep assessments and concrete practices.

Teachers with the Teacher

First, let's remember the point of departure of our meditation: as Christians committed to the educational task, we have an important *responsibility*, and at the same time, an *opportunity* to make our contribution. For this reason, it is necessary *to succeed* in the objectives which are to be prioritized, based on a wisdom matured in the experience of meeting with the Lord. For this purpose, it would not be superfluous to ask ourselves the fundamental question: *for what purpose do we educate*? Why does the Church, why do Christian communities, invest time, assets, and energy in a task that is not directly *religious*? Why do we have schools, and not hair salons, veterinary clinics, or tourist agencies? Perhaps as a business? There will be those who think so, but the reality of many of our schools puts the lie to this affirmation. Would it be to exercise an influence in society, an influence from which we subsequently hope for some benefit?

It is possible that some schools offer this *product* to their *clients*: contacts, environment, *excellence*. But neither is this the reason for which the ethical and evangelical imperative pushes us to offer this service. The only reason we engage ourselves in the field of education is the *hope for a new mankind*, in another possible world.

It is the hope which springs from Christian wisdom, which in the Resurrected One reveals to us the divine stature to which we are called. With the language and the

theology of his time, Estrada laid out clearly this purpose
of the educational task from the Christian perspective:

Do you see the men of this century striving because of
an inexhaustible longing for perfection? We also love
progress and perfection, but a perfection fit for man
in the totality of his destiny and of his moral nature.
Science is excellent, and I applaud and love her, because it is a law that men command nature; but it is
also our law to aspire to noumenal and immortal ends;
and the purification of the soul and its union with God
require the adoption of supernatural means as well as
ends. The condition and supreme object of all progress
is the restoration of the supernatural in man by virtue
of Christ. Napoleon guessed it: to educate is to create.

All this is not mere poetry. Indeed many of the current
values in our society lose sight of this inclusive and tran-
scendent truth which constitutes the sum of men and community. School can simply be the transmitter of these *values*
or the cradle of other new ones; but this assumes a community that believes and hopes, a community that loves, a
community that is really gathered in the name of the Resurrected One. Before the plans and the curricula, before
defining the specific modality of codes and regulations, *it
is necessary to know what it is that we want to generate.* I
also know that for this purpose the entire teaching community needs to involve itself, share forcefully in one selfsame viewpoint, becoming passionately committed to the
project of Jesus and drawing everyone to that same side.

Many institutions promote the formation of wolves,
rather than of brothers; they educate for competence and

success at the cost of others, with a few weak *ethical* norms, sustained by impoverished committees that try to mitigate the corrosive destructiveness of certain practices that will of *necessity* have to be carried out. In many classrooms, the strong and the quick are rewarded, and the weak and slow are disregarded. In many it is encouraged to be *number one* in results, and not in compassion. Now then, our specifically Christian contribution is *an education that witnesses to and realizes another way of being human.* But this is not possible if we limit ourselves simply *to endure* the *rain*, *floods*, and *winds*, if we remain in mere criticism and we take pleasure in being *outside* the standards that we denounce. The possibility of a different mankind . . . requires a *positive action*; if not, it will always be *another* that is simply invoked, while *this* one continues to be in force and ever more firmly established.

I consider that a more active posture inevitably requires that we succeed in overcoming *some conflicts* that, rather than clarifying, paralyze us. Certain rigid antagonisms end up exaggerating the ambiguities that *give rise* to potentialities toward those orientations that we consider more negative. A real, decisive and responsible compromise invites us to advance in our discernment and to overcome certain clichés that are very rooted in our communities. To this end, then, I propose to you *three challenges* that are interconnected: to posit that the end of our task is *yielding fruit*, without ignoring the results; favoring that which is *given freely*, without losing *efficiency*; and creating a space where excellence does not imply a loss of *solidarity*.

"Fruits" and "Results"

Our task has one objective: to produce something in the students who have been entrusted to us; to provoke a change, a growth in wisdom. We hope that after passing through our classrooms, the children or young people will have lived through a transformation, that they have more knowledge, new sentiments, and at the same time attainable ideals. For the instructor who wishes to be a teacher of wisdom, it is not sufficient to "fulfill one's obligations" with verbosity and attention. The gaze goes beyond necessary competence and professional probity; it centers rather in what it arouses in the pupils who are the *raison d'être* of their vocation.

This *transformation* we desire and hope for, on which we stake everything we have, has multiple aspects which must be united in order to suggest something better. In a way that perhaps is schematic but useful for understanding, we can locate them in two dimensions that are called, reciprocally: *"to produce results" and "to yield fruit"*.

What do both objectives imply? *"To yield fruit"* is a metaphor that we take from agriculture; it is the way in which the new presents itself in the world of living beings. We could also use the image of *engendering*: to give life to a new being. Whatever it may be, vegetable or animal, the idea points to an interior process in the subjects. Fruit is formed from the same identity as that of the living being, it nourishes itself with those forces that have already come to form a part of its being, it enriches itself with the multiple internal identifications and is something *unique*, surprising, original. Nature does not produce two fruits that are exactly identical. In the same way, a subject that *yields fruits* is someone who has matured his creativity in a process of liberty, gestating something new departing from the truth received, accepted, and assimilated.

How do we connect this with our concrete work? A teacher who wisely aims to make his task *yield fruits* will never limit himself to hoping for something predetermined, accepting that the subject adjusts himself to a mold that is considered desirable. He will not dismiss the different and that which challenges some of his habitual practices. He will not deceive himself with fulfillment that is hyper-compliant and unquestioned by the students. He knows that a question from a student is worth more than a thousand answers, and he will encourage searching without failing to be attentive to the risks which this implies. In the face of questioning and rebellion he will not vanquish or impose, but rather promote responsibility through an intelligent critique, from an open and flexible disposition that confidently *learns by teaching and teaches by learning.* And when he encounters a failure or an error, far from denying it or noting it triumphantly or bitterly, he will patiently take up the process once more at the point where it encountered an obstacle or detour, promoting patient apprenticeship and himself learning in the process.

For its part, *the metaphor of the "production of results"* belongs to the field of industry, of serial and calculable effectiveness. A result can be foreseen, planned, and measured. It implies a control over the steps that are being taken. A set of perfectly determined actions that will have a *predictable* effect.

A society that tends to convert man into a marionette of production and consumption always opts for results. It needs control, it cannot make room for innovation without seriously compromising its objectives and without increasing the degree of conflict that already exists. It prefers that the other be completely predictable in order to acquire the maximum benefit with the minimum of expense.

But *wisdom does not only imply maturation in the order of content and values, but also in that of skills.* All true transformation with a view to this other possible world to which we aspire implies also knowing how to do, an instrumental competence that is necessary to incorporate, understanding its logic. Our students have the right, above all, to their own autonomy and uniqueness; but also to develop skills that are socially recognized, proven, with a view to being able to express their desires and contributions in the real world. The teacher who is rooted in Christian wisdom does not disdain the necessary effectiveness that he ought to attain, with all the effort that this implies for him and for his students. He knows that in order to pass from *good intentions* to attainment it is necessary to traverse an arduous path of technique, discipline, economy of effort, incorporation of the experiences of others, and he is able to persevere with his students along this road despite the fact that he as much as they would sometimes prefer to take shortcuts or stay in some backwater.

The problem is rooted in the fact that *many times we Christians have dissociated "fruits" from "results".* In this way, we neglect our formation, we lower the level when it would be better for the students that we find the means to motivate and sustain their effort; we settle for managing a good climate and establishing good connections, instead of constructing a dynamic of creativity and productivity upon this framework. Or, on the contrary, we take refuge in stereotypical behavior, correctly formulated beliefs, expressions according to the norm . . . all starting from a freedom that is more "domesticated" than fortified, thinking that this way we have "educated"!

There is nothing worse than a Christian educational institution that is conceived in uniformity and calculation, in "sausage-making" fashion, so crudely caricatured in the film *The Wall* some years ago. Our objective is not only to form "useful individuals for society", *but to educate persons who can transform it*! This will not be achieved by sacrificing the maturation of skills, the deepening of knowledge, the diversification of tastes, because, finally, *the neglect of these "results" will not yield "new men and women", but flaccid puppets of the consumer society.*

It is a question of resolving the polarities, integrating them with each other: "to educate for fruits" while providing all the possible tools so that this fruit becomes more concrete in every moment, in an effective way, *"producing results"*. From the objectivity of truth let us propose open, inspiring ideals and models, without imposing the format which we have found to harness this dynamic, developing in turn the interventions necessary so that the children can mobilize their choices. We prefer free and responsible pupils, capable of questioning, deciding, getting things right or making mistakes yet continuing on their path, and not mere replicas of our own right answers . . . or of our

errors. And precisely for that reason, let us be able to make
them gain the confidence and security that springs from the
experience of their own creativity, their own skill, their own
ability to put things into practice and carry through their
own orientations successfully.

This assumes seriously believing in every occasion for
dialogue, in the power of the word. Not an idealized word:
a word that can encourage and urge, open doors and establish limits, invite and forgive. All of which supposes also
certain extremely difficult virtues: humility to know how
to relativize one's own attitudes, patience to know how to
wait for the proper moment for the other, and magnanimity
to persevere and not diminish the effort to give one's best.

Magnanimity with Efficiency

Indeed, we Christians try to favor the *rule of generosity* in
our schools. In the first place, for its intrinsic value: it is
the *sign par excellence of the love of God and of the love between human beings according to the unconditional model
of Christ*. And in the second place, because we know and
suffer the consequences of the *extension of economic criteria to all human activity*.

If we understand efficiency to mean obtaining maximum
results with a minimum of expense of energy and resources,
it is obvious that in providing an education for the purpose
of yielding fruit, value, and freedom, we will have to re-
think all these relations. Undoubtedly, the energy invested
in our children and young people will be immense, and the
results will not always be those we desire. What is more,

in the final analysis, the fruit will depend upon each individual, a point that does not excuse us from evaluating
our task.

A standard of efficiency left to itself would lead us *to
invest more where we have the greatest guarantee of success.*
Exactly like the current success-oriented, privatizing model.
Why spend on those who will never emerge from their
hopelessness, asks the investor who is looking for a return before anything else. What sense does it make to invest more and more so that the *slowest or most troubled*
can find their path? Why do the *least gifted* (and now it is
desired also to take account of genetics to determine the
have-nots) squander the goods of the community, since in
any case they will never reach the requisite levels?

But this logic of bad pedagogical humanism is upset
when we consider the nucleus of our faith: the Son of God
became man and died on the Cross for the salvation of
men. What is the proportion between the *investment* made
by God and the object of this expenditure? We could say
without being irreverent: there is nothing more inefficient
than God. To sacrifice his Son for mankind, and mankind
sinful and ungrateful to the present day. . . . There is no
doubt: the logic of the history of salvation is a *logic of
disinterested generosity.* It is not measured by *should* and
must, nor even by the merits claimed.

Because we read in the Gospel that the mustard seed,
such a small seed, becomes an enormous bush and we capture the disproportion between the action and its effect;
then we know that *we are not the owners of the gift* and we
try to be *careful and efficient stewards.* We must be efficient

in our mission because it is a matter of the Lord's work, and not primarily of our own. The Word which is sown yields fruit according to its own potentiality and according to the soil in which it falls. For these reasons, the sower will not execute his work with laziness or carelessness. The correspondence to the divine free gift is man's adoration and gratitude; adoration and gratitude that imply a consummate respect for the wisdom shared, for the precious gift of the Word and of words.

Let us not be misled: efficiency as a value in itself, as an ultimate standard, does not by any means hold up. When in the field of business, today, efficiency is emphasized, it is clear that it is to maximize earnings. However: *we must be efficient so that the "earnings" can be given freely. Efficiency at the service of an educational task that is truly free.* I am not referring here to fees and contributions (if we could find the formula so that the poorest of the poor could exercise their civic right to choose our schools because they are free!) but rather of *a fundamental attitude* that predominates. Neither the meaning nor the efficiency of our task is defined principally by the resources used and their calculation; but precisely for this reason we must give the best on our part. Jesus also took account of this dimension: it was not for nothing that he taught the parable of the talents. . . .

This commits us seriously, as Christian teachers, to give freely and with care what freely and carefully we have received; in the same way it must also form part of the *content* of what we transmit. The teacher who wishes to make Christian wisdom his principle of life and the meaning and content of his vocation will have to pay attention to the climate in the classroom and the entire institution, in the attitudes he assumes and promotes, in the style of daily exchanges, seeking to capture in all that an atmosphere of care and unstinting generosity. Never an atmosphere of calculated interactions, measured and self-interested, although he may sometimes feel that temptation to hedge his dedication. Nor an atmosphere of neglect and disdain for the assets, time, sensibility, and effort of each of the stakeholders of his enterprise: students, colleagues, collaborators, families. Although the profoundly unsupportive culture in which we live prompts him daily to shrug his shoulders saying "what is it to me", he will feel deeply responsible not to squander what belongs to everyone: his knowledge, his school along with all those who participate in it, the teaching vocation.

And with this, we arrive at our third and final challenge.

The Excellence of Solidarity

The standard that breaks with the logic of competitive individualism is, finally, that of *solidarity*. Here is where the contribution of Christian educators can become more critical and relevant because, beyond speeches, the *"ethics" of competition* (which is no more than an implementation of reason to justify force) has full currency in our society.

To educate for solidarity supposes not only teaching to be *good* and *generous*, to take up collections, to participate in public good works, to support foundations and NGOs. It is precisely to create a new mentality that thinks in terms of community, of the priority of the lives of all and each one above the appropriation of goods by a few.

A mentality born in that old teaching of social doctrine of the Church regarding the *social function of property or the universal destiny of goods* as a primary right, prior to private property, to the point that the latter is subordinated to the former. This mentality must become body and mind of our institutions, it must cease to be a dead letter in order to express itself in realities that configure another culture and another society. It is urgent to fight for the rescue of concrete persons, sons and daughters of God, above any pretension to the indiscriminate use of the goods of the earth.

Solidarity, then, more than an *affective* or individual *attitude*, is *a way of understanding and living activity and human society*. It must be reflected in ideas, practices, sentiments, structures, and institutions; it implies a global outline with regard to the various dimensions of existence; it carries a commitment to express itself in real relations among groups and persons; it demands not only *private* or *public* activity that seeks to alleviate the consequences of social imbalances but also the search for paths that prevent those imbalances from occurring, paths that will not be simple, much less celebrated by those who have opted for a model of egotistical accumulation and who have benefited from it.

This essential solidarity becomes a type of *brand name*, a *certification of authenticity* of the Christian style, of that form of life and that way of thinking about the educational enterprise. We have no need of any ideology critical of Christianism in order to put forward our innovation. *Either we are able to form men and women with this new mentality or we will have failed in our mission.* This will also

imply reviewing the standards that have guided our actions
to the present day. It is appropriate to ask ourselves:

Where, among ourselves, is that solidarity as a part of
the culture? We cannot deny that there exist many signs
of bigheartedness among our people; but why do they not
express themselves in a more just and fraternal society?
Where, then, is the sign of the Resurrected One in the country that we have constructed?

Perhaps it is a matter, once again, of a *disconnect between ends and means*. But this affirmation deserves to be
developed in a little more detail. I already mentioned that
today there is much talk of *"excellence"*, sometimes from
a nonsupportive and elitist perspective. Those who *can* demand *excellence* because *they pay for it*. This, lamentably, is
a claim too frequently heard to be disregarded. The problem is that it is never seriously asked what happens with
those who *cannot*, and much less, what are the causes for
which some *can* and others *cannot*. Like so many other
things that issue from a long chain of human actions and
decisions, this situation is considered as a *datum*, something as natural as the rain or the wind.

Now, what would happen if we reversed the question and
proposed to achieve an *excellence of solidarity*? The dictionary of the Royal Academy defines excellence as "superior
quality or goodness that makes something worthy of singular appreciation and esteem". Going further, we know
that in ancient Greece excellence was a concept that was
very close to *virtue*: perfection in some socially valued order. Not only *appreciation*, but that which deserves it: the
superior ability which manifests itself in the quality of the

action. In this way, to speak about the *excellence of solidarity* implies, at the first level, *postulating solidarity as a desirable good*, raising the value of this disposition and this practice. It carries within itself doing well that which concerns us and takes as a starting point the spirit of the mission that is proper to every teacher, that begins—as Jesus himself indicated upon washing the feet of his disciples—with a profound personal conversion, affective and effective, that translates into witness: "If I then, your Lord and Teacher, have washed your feet, you also ought to wash one another's feet. For I have given you an example, that you also should do as I have done to you" (Jn 13:14–15).

In the second place, *to perfect this solidarity*. There are moments in which we are asked to give more, to advance beyond what we were working on and devoting ourselves to by virtue of the obligations or demands of pressing reality. We could talk about a *superficial* solidarity and a *fertile* solidarity. We know the first: mere declarations, a show of generosity, prompt help that sometimes hypocritically hides the true root of the problem. . . . Or, without going so far, mere sentimentality, lack of vision, superficiality and naïveté. On the contrary, the excellence of solidarity implies a whole way of thinking and living, as we said before; and further: an effective concern that our practice of solidarity really produces a change.

Here we imagine a possible reason for what appears to be an *impotence of solidarity. It is not sufficient to be "good" and "generous": it is necessary to be intelligent, capable, effective*. We Christians have put so much emphasis on the rectitude and sincerity of our love, on conversion of the heart, that sometimes we have neglected objective success in the process of our fraternal charity. As if the only thing that mattered were the intention . . . and appropriate interventions are ignored. This is not enough; it is not enough for our most needy brothers, victims of injustice and exclusion, whom "the interior of our hearts" does not help in their necessity. Nor is it enough for ourselves: a useless solidarity only serves to alleviate the feeling of guilt a bit. What is needed is *elevated goals . . . and appropriate means.*

Thus we see, finally, that there is no reason to oppose solidarity and excellence, if we understand them in this way. A teacher who wisely is rooted in the model of Jesus of Nazareth will be capable of discerning in his own heart the motives of his commitment and self-giving, and will find in his vocation, in his personal abilities and in an active preoccupation with formation and personal communitarian reflection, the way to generate a change in his charges, in pursuit of a fraternal and inclusive society. And he will do it with concrete initiatives that range from the type of treatment that he maintains and promotes with each of his students to his participation in the educational community in a more integral sense; from his spirit of comradeship and solidarity in work to the firmness of his ethical and spiritual options, always attempting to discern, with a gaze that combines intelligence and love, the best of each of his children in order to promote in them the *excellence* of virtue, the personal vocation through which they will be called to live and sow the Kingdom.

In this way we arrive at the end of our reflection. Thinking about what we can and should contribute to our country today we put at the center of our consideration the *dimension of wisdom* which the Gospel reveals in Jesus.

An ideal that is worthy of presiding over the best of our education efforts!

Christian wisdom: truth, life and way illuminated us at the moment of discerning some ethical orientations and historical options for our educational task.

Not to remain stuck in words but to construct on the rock will mean to take ourselves seriously in the sense of our mission: *if in our schools we do not develop another way of being human, another culture and another society, we are wasting our time.* To advance this task, I propose the challenge of *overcoming certain antinomies* that prevent us from growing:

First, to decide to produce in our children and young people a transformation that yields fruits of liberty, self-determination, creativity and—at the same time—displays results in terms of really operative abilities and knowledge. Our objective is not to form islands of peace in the midst of an atomized society but to educate persons with the capacity of transforming that society. Hence, *"fruits"* and *"results"*.

To this end, to opt unhesitatingly for the logic of the gospel: logic of magnanimity, of the unconditional gift, but trying to administer our resources with the greatest responsibility and seriousness. Only in this way will we be able to distinguish the free gift from the indifferent and the careless. *Disinterested generosity with efficiency.*

And finally, overcoming the destructive ethic of the competition of *all against all*, to carry forward the practice of a solidarity that takes aim at the roots of egotism in an effective way, not remaining in mere declamations and complaints, but putting our best abilities at the service of this ideal. Elevated goals and appropriate means: the *excellence of solidarity.*

Teachers with the Teacher: witnesses of a new wisdom, new and eternal, because the Kingdom that God has put in motion in our history calls us always to hope for more than all the searches and attempts that we could possibly dream of. In this universal innovation we can be seeds of a better mankind, a sign of what is to come.

Our vocation is nothing less than this. Have we forgotten our fragility? On the contrary, it moves us to allow ourselves to be carried, with the confidence of little ones, by the strength of the One who sustains and encourages us, who makes all things new: the Holy Spirit. Spirit who makes the living Jesus present in every Eucharist that is celebrated, as an inexhaustible love of the Father; gathering us and sending us boldly to forge among us all a country that educates.

—Buenos Aires, at Easter
of the year of our Lord 2004

Key to Reading
for Working Individually or in Groups

⌐ Let's reflect

"If we look at *Jesus, incarnate Wisdom of God,* we will be able to realize that difficulties become challenges, challenges call forth hope and generate happiness in knowing yourselves to be the architects of something new. All this surely impels us to continue giving the best of ourselves."

FOR PERSONAL REFLECTION

—In whom will I find a model of wisdom throughout my life?

—How do I react in the face of challenges?

—What is the best I have to give in my teaching vocation?

FOR WORK IN GROUPS

—What are the greatest challenges confronting our culture?

—Where do we find wisdom in the attitudes of our society?

—What could be the innovation that we have to contribute as a Church?

📨 Let's read

"He saw a poor widow put in two copper coins. And he said, 'Truly I tell you, this poor widow has put in more than all of them; for they all contributed out of their abundance, but she out of her poverty put in all the living that she had.'"

—*Luke 21:2–4*

📨 Let's think

"It is because of this that loyalty to the educational aims of the Catholic school demands constant self-criticism and return to basic principles, to the motives which inspire the Church's involvement in education. They do not provide a quick answer to contemporary problems, but they give a direction which can begin to solve them. Account has to be taken of new pedagogical insights and collaboration with others, irrespective of religious allegiance, who work honestly for the true development of mankind."

—*The Catholic School, 67*

📨 Let's review our task

It is clear that the only motive we have for doing something in the field of education is the *hope for a new mankind*, in another possible world. It is hope that springs from Christian wisdom, which in the Resurrected One reveals to us the divine stature to which we are called. Our specifically Christian contribution is *an education that witnesses to and brings about another way of being human.*

And to this end it is necessary to overcome three contradictions that, in turn, confront us with three challenges:

—Fruits and results

Our objective is not only to form "useful individuals for society", but *to educate persons who can transform it.*

• What is it necessary to renovate in our educational communities in order to form genuinely free and responsible persons?

• What incentivizes creativity and initiative in our students?

• What *percentage* of the following attitudes do we find in our teaching life?

Dialogue
Humility
Patience
Magnanimity

—Generosity with efficiency

As Christian teachers, we know that we are not the masters of the gift we have received and we try to be careful and efficient administrators. We must be efficient in our mission because it is a matter of the work of the Lord, and not primarily of our own.

• How do we prepare ourselves to transmit the gospel message in our specific task?

• What is peculiar to the Christian educator, that is, what distinguishes him from one who is not?

• How do we efficiently promote this spirit of openhanded generosity in our educational institution?

—Excellence in solidarity

Solidarity, more than an affective or individual attitude, is a way of understanding and living human activity and society. It becomes a kind of *certificate of authenticity* of the Christian way of carrying forward the educational mission.

• Among ourselves, where is this solidarity embedded into culture?

• Why do the many signs of generosity we perceive in our country not express themselves in a more just and fraternal society?

• What channels of solidarity exist within our educational community?

Let us pray

Let us pray with Psalm 62:

For God alone my soul waits in silence;
    from him comes my salvation.
He only is my rock and my salvation,
    my fortress; I shall not be greatly moved.

How long will you set upon a man
    to shatter him, all of you,
    like a leaning wall, a tottering fence?
They only plan to thrust him down from his eminence.
    They take pleasure in falsehood.

They bless with their mouths,
  but inwardly they curse.   *Selah*

For God alone my soul waits in silence,
  for my hope is from him.
He only is my rock and my salvation,
  my fortress; I shall not be shaken.
On God rests my deliverance and my honor;
  my mighty rock, my refuge is God.

Trust in him at all times, O people;
  pour out your heart before him;
God is a refuge for us.   *Selah*

Men of low estate are but a breath,
  men of high estate are a delusion;
in the balances they go up;
  they are together lighter than a breath.
Put no confidence in extortion,
  set no vain hopes on robbery;
  if riches increase, set not your heart on them.

Once God has spoken;
  twice have I heard this:
that power belongs to God;
  and that to you, O Lord, belongs steadfast love.
For you repay a man
  according to his work.

3

An Opportunity to Mature

A New Opportunity of Providence

Dear educators: Once more, the central festival of all Chris
tians provides the occasion to embark upon a reflection on
the task that has brought us together. We try to take the
pulse of the times in which we live, and to understand how
we can recreate our spiritual experience in a way that re-
sponds accurately to the questions, anxieties and hopes of
our times.

This effort is really indispensable. In the first place, beginning with the most obvious, because we are immersed
in a situation in which we see with ever greater clarity the
consequences of the errors that have been committed and
the demands that the reality of our country imposes on
us. We have the sensation that *providence has given us a
new opportunity* to establish ourselves in a truly just and
supportive community, where all persons are respected in
their dignity and promoted in their liberty, in order to fulfill their destiny as daughters and sons of God.

This opportunity is also a challenge. We have in our hands
an immense responsibility, derived precisely from the requirement not to squander the chance that has been offered
to us. It is obvious as I point out to you, dear educators,

that your share in this undertaking is very important. It is a task that is replete with difficulties and whose development will surely generate dialogue and even, why not say so, require arduous discussions which have for their objective the contribution to the common good from an open and truly democratic perspective, overcoming the tendency—so much our own—to mutual exclusions and the discrediting (or condemnation) of whoever thinks or acts differently.

I still dare to insist: we Argentines have a long history of mutual intolerance. Even the teaching we have received in school was articulated around the shedding of blood between compatriots, in whichever of the versions —whichever happened to be the *official* one at the moment—of the history of the nineteenth century. With that background, in the school narrative that considered the National Organization as the overcoming of those antinomies, we entered as a people into the twentieth century, but only to continue excluding one another, banning one another, assassinating one another, bombing one another, shooting one another, repressing one another, and "disappearing" one another. Those of us who are able to remember know that the use of these verbs that I have just chosen is not exactly metaphorical.

Will we be in a condition to learn now? Will we be able to mature as a community so that at last the deplorable prophecy of Martín Fierro about the brothers who are devoured by outsiders or, even worse, who devour one another, will cease to have a painful prevalence?

Other observations have shown us, thanks be to God, that there are produced all kinds of choices and initiatives among us that promote life and solidarity, that clamor for justice, that try to search for the truth. It will be in these personal and social energies that we will have to delve in order to respond to the call of God to construct, once and for all and by his grace, a country of brothers.

But in addition, the effort to read the signs of the times in order to understand what God is calling us to do in each historical situation is required as well by the very structure of the Christian faith. I dare to say that without this permanent exercise, our Christian vocation—as Christian teachers, pastors, witnesses of the resurrection in the multiple dimensions of human life—deteriorates to the point of losing its true transformative value. *It is not possible to incline one's ear to the word of salvation outside the place where it sets out for this encounter with us, that is, in the concrete human history* in which the Lord became incarnate and in which he founded his Church to preach the gospel "to the close of the age" (Mt 28:20).

A Mature Community Puts Life First

From our ecclesial communities, we are aware that we Argentines are passing through times of change and that today more than ever prayer and reflection have become necessary, ordered to a serious spiritual and pastoral discernment.

Particularly, I would like to call your attention to all those who are in charge of the task of *accompanying children and young people in their process of maturation.* I believe that it is critical to try to approach the reality these children live in our society, and ask ourselves what role we play in it.

If we want to take reality as our point of departure, we cannot fail to place in the middle of the scene two painful incidents that together have shaken society, but particularly young people, and those who are close to them. I refer to the tragedy of Carmen de Patagones and the terrible December 30 in the neighborhood of Once of the province of Buenos Aires. Two very different incidents in themselves, but ones that have a common message for our community: what is happening to our children? Or rather, what is happening with ourselves, that we do not take responsibility for the situation of abandonment and isolation in which our children find themselves? How is it that we have become aware of the problems of adolescents only when one of them suffers a crisis that leads him to kill his companions with a firearm stolen from his father? How is it that we take note of the apathy of those whose task is to take care of our children only when almost two hundred people, in their great majority children, adolescents and young people, are sacrificed in a terrible nightclub accident in the name of business, carelessness, and irresponsibility? It is obviously not our place to determine responsibility, although we know that it is essential that responsibility be assigned and that each be required to accept it. It is not good to dilute human actions and omissions which have had such terrible consequences in a kind of collective guilt. As we prayed in the Mass of the month of the tragedy, "we ask justice (of God). We ask that his humble people not be mocked by worldly cleverness; that his generous hand put things in their proper place and do justice. The wound is painful. Nobody has the right to experiment with children and young people. They are the hope of the nation and we must take care of them with decisive responsibility."

Even so, and while we are confident that looking beyond political opportunism, responsibility and seriousness take precedence in a matter which ought to have been settled long before (the common good in its most basic expression, the very life of the citizenry), *we need to open our eyes and reexamine our own ideas, sentiments, acts, and omissions in the field of the care, the advancement, and the education of children and adolescents.* Because another risk that can be defined is to relegate the problem to a question of control in recreational facilities, in the same way that, a few months ago, the discussion about situations of violence that is reflected in the school could have slipped into a mere instruction of psychodiagnostics and for the children from a medical-type perspective, psychopathologizing. And I am not minimizing the importance of guaranteeing the safety conditions of the locales, or the undeniable contribution of health professionals. I am simply urging that we be well aware that things are never isolated from each other, and all of us (parents, educators, pastors . . .) have in our hands *the responsibility and also the possibility of making of this world something that is much more habitable for our children.*

At this point, I would like to reiterate to you some ideas that I shared with many of you in the Teachers Forum last October.

We are all aware of the ever mounting difficulties that hinder us from walking beside our children outside our

educational institutions. As I told you in the forum, the
pressures of the market, with its offerings of consumption
and ruthless competition, the lack of economic, social, psychological, and moral resources, the ever greater gravity of
the risks to be avoided . . . all that makes it an uphill battle for families to fulfill their function, and *makes schools
ever more isolated in the task of containing, sustaining, and
promoting the human development of their students.*

This solitude ends up being experienced, inevitably, as
excessive demands. I know that you, dear teachers, are having to carry on your shoulders not only that for which you
prepared, but also a multitude of explicit or tacit demands
that exhaust you. Add to this the various communication
mediums—one is not sure whether they help or confuse
things more—when dealing with extremely delicate questions with the same lack of discretion as the display of inti-
macies on the movie screen, in print advertisements, in the
pages of the newspaper, intermingled with advertisements
for things that are utterly disconnected from reality. And
all that, while we appear to be becoming a society of ever
greater control, in which everybody mistrusts everybody;
and at the same time, with the recent attention legitimately
being given to many forms of negligence and abuse, people
cling to the bad habit of ventilating their condemnations
without sufficiently checking sources; as well as unscrupu-
lous people who simply see institutions as opportunities
for financial gain at any cost.

And then? What do you have to do, you who are over-
burdened and tired? Is one in the right to say, "my task is
to teach such and such a discipline, I am not going to offer
my body to be flogged, let others take care of their own re-

sponsibilities"? And yes, let us hope that each would carry out his duties. But, as I said some months ago, the teacher cannot limit herself to be the *second mother* that she was in other times, if there wasn't before that a *first*. I am sure that we all like to remember how, when we were little, we could play on the sidewalk, adequately fed, and loved, in families where well-being, affection and care were the stuff of every day. I also know that more than once we have tried to discuss when things stopped being like that, who began it, who degraded education, who severed the relation between education and work, who weakened the family, who undermined authority, who pulverized the state, who led us to institutional anomy, who corrupted ideals, who deflated the utopias. . . . We can analyze all this endlessly, debate, opine . . . but what is not up for discussion is that you daily confront boys and girls of flesh and blood, with possibilities, desires, fears, and real lacks. Children who are there, in body and soul, as they are and as they live, before an adult, demanding, hoping, criticizing, begging in their way, infinitely alone, needy, terrified, persistently confiding in you although sometimes they do it with apparent indifference, disdain, or anger; attentive to see whether someone will offer them something different . . . or will slam one more door in their face.

An immense responsibility, that requires of us not only an ethical decision, not only a conscious and strenuous commitment, but also and more fundamentally, *an adequate level of personal maturity.*

Maturity that sometimes appears to be pretty scarce in our Argentine society, always needing to start from zero, as if those who came before us had never existed, always looking for the means of leaping the divide, although what unites us is staring us in the face, always opposing one another with doubts, throwing the stone and hiding the hand, whistling under our breath and looking the other way when push comes to shove, declaiming patriotism and passion for justice while we pass the envelope under the table or get a friend to let us cut in line. . . .

It seems that a meditation on maturity will do all of us good. Not only so that we mature as we meditate, but in order to see ourselves with eyes that are more open (perhaps as our adolescents see us?) and, as a result, we begin to change even if it be the conduct and attitudes that are most within our grasp.

Maturity Is More than Growth

It is not easy to define what *maturity* consists of. Above all, because more than a concept, *maturity* seems to be a metaphor. Taken from fruit farming? I do not know. If it were so, we would have to point out immediately that there is a fundamental difference between apples and peaches, and human beings. While the full development (because that is what we are talking about) of fruit is a process that depends directly on certain determined genetic programs of the organism and of suitable ambient conditions (climate, the action of insects, birds, and winds for the pollination of flowers, humidity, the soil's nutrients . . .), in the case of human maturity, it is not a matter only of genetics and nutrition. Unless we consider man as a living being that differs in no way from others (amoebas, cactus . . .).

Sometimes, when one reads certain *scientific* revelations, one is left with the impression that genes determine that one's first tooth falls out at the age of five, that one has a bad time at school, that one is poor, that one is sociable, that one day one will kill his mother-in-law, and finally that he will die of a heart attack at the age of forty-some years, all almost at the same level as having straight or curly hair.

But if *maturity* were only the development of something previously contained in the genetic code, really there would not be much to do. The dictionary of the Royal Academy gives us the second meaning of *maturity*: "good judgment or prudence, good sense". And here we find ourselves in a very different universe from that of biology. Because prudence, good judgment and good sense do not depend on merely quantitative factors of growth, but on a whole chain of elements which are synthesized in the interior of the person. To be more exact, *in the center of his freedom.*

So maturity, from this point of view (which appears much more interesting and rich for our reflection), could be understood as *the capacity to use our liberty in a "sensible"*, *"prudent" manner*. Note that with this, we flee not only biological reductionism but even from the psychological perspective, to embrace an ethical consideration. Take note: it is not a question of choosing one or the other focus. Without a definite genetic program we cannot be human, and without the development of faculties that are the object of psychology we will not be able to talk about maturity in the ethical sense. But precisely because the human implies this multiplicity of dimensions, I want to underscore the difference: it is not my purview, as a pastor, to "give classes" of psychology, but rather to propose to you a series of thoughts that have to do with the orientation of our free acts.

If we speak about good sense and prudence, then words, dialogue, even teaching will have much to do with maturity. Because in order to start to work in this sensible manner, one has to have accumulated many experiences, made many choices, tried many responses to the challenges of life. It is obvious that there is no *prudence* without time. At first, then, still very close to the psychological or even biological perspective, *maturity implies time.*

But let us again take up the mature person as someone who has use of his liberty in a given manner. What, we ask ourselves immediately, is this manner? Because here another problem opens up: is there a kind of *tribunal of maturity?* Who determines when something is *sensible and prudent?* The others (whoever they might be)? Or each one, from his experience and orientation? If in the first instance we have to relate maturity with time, then next we will have to place ourselves in the *conflict between the individual and everyone else.* Liberty in time, liberty in society.

This, then, is the trajectory that I propose to you. A trajectory that, as we will see, will permit us to understand human maturity in an open perspective. Because at the end we will find ourselves with the final dimension of maturity: the divine invitation to transcend the horizon of the intersubjective and social in order to open ourselves to the religious, that is to say, the *ethical maturity of sanctity.*

But let's not get ahead of ourselves: the reflection is still *green.*

Maturity Requires Experience in Time

For something to cease to be *green* and come truly to be *mature* it is essential not to hurry. How many times have we been disappointed by fine-looking fruit with little flavor! And we said, "it is refrigerated" . . . that is, it was not given the necessary time to reach its peak.

Allowing for the obvious differences, human maturation, in its ethical dimension, also requires time. Psychologists from diverse schools concur, beyond their differences, that moral conscience develops through a process that implies stages and various movements, traversed necessarily through time.

It is like this: to come to a point of maturity, that is, in order to be capable of truly free and responsible decisions, *it is necessary for us to have been given [to be given] time.*

Within time a number of essential operations occur to form freedom. For example, the ability to wait. We know that "I want it now" is the motto of small children and of those who we consider not to have matured appropriately. It is probably one of the most important things that we have to learn. If nothing more, because the step from immediate satisfaction to waiting, the symbolizing and mediation of reasoned action, is one of the factors that define us as humans. Among us, stimulus does not necessarily awaken an immediate and automatic response. *It is precisely in the space between the stimulus and the response that we have constructed all of culture.*

This implies a long road of apprenticeship, based on abilities that mature from the biological and the psychic.

Sometimes we tend to imagine the figure of the *"old sage"* as someone who has arrived at a certain *impassibility*. Beyond certain accents that are typical of the oriental worldview present in these images, it is true that this distancing from things and from pressures is one of the aspects that stands out in everyone who can be connected with *good sense* and *prudence*. At least, as far as the ability not to be guided by first impulses. The prudent, mature man *thinks* before acting. *He takes his time.*

Will it be obvious to note that all that implies a series of operations that are very difficult in the present *digital culture*? The time of reflection is by no means the time of perception and immediate response of computer games, of *on-line* communications, of operations of all kinds in which the important thing is to "be connected" and to "act fast". It is not a question of forbidding children from playing with electronic machines but to find the way of generating in them the ability to differentiate various logics and not to apply uniquely digital speed to all spheres of life.

We will also try to be alert to our own tendencies toward immediate stimulus-response. To give an example: the rise —originating in the media—of opinion: everyone has opinions about everything, whether they know anything about it or not, whether or not they have a basis for judgment. How to allow ourselves space to think, to dialogue, to exchange opinions in order to construct solid and responsible positions, when daily we nurse a style of thought that is provisional, shaky, and unconcerned about coherence? It is obvious that we cannot withdraw from being a part of the information society in which we live, but what we can do is to take the time to analyze, unfold possibilities, visualize consequences, exchange points of view, listen to other voices . . . and proceed to construct, in this way, the discursive framework on which it will be possible to produce prudent decisions.

To take the time to wait is also *to take the time to build*. Really important things require time: to learn a job or a profession, to know a person and establish a lasting relationship of love or friendship, to know how to distinguish the important from the essential. . . .

You know very well that there are things that cannot be hurried in the classroom. Each child has his time, each group has its rhythm. . . . Last year I spoke to you about the difference between *yielding fruit* and *producing results*. Well, one of the differences is precisely the quality of time implied in each of these objectives. In the production of results, one can foresee and even rationalize or render time efficient; in waiting for fruit, one can not. It is just that, a wait: time, rhythm, are not in our hands. It implies humility, patience, attention and listening.

The Gospel offers us a very beautiful image of the Holy Family *taking its time*, allowing Jesus to mature, growing "in wisdom and in stature, and in favor with God and man" (Lk 2:52). *God himself made time the principal axis of his plan of salvation.* The waiting of us, his people, is concentrated and symbolized in Mary's and Joseph's waiting for this child who *takes his time in* maturing his identity and his mission, and later, as a man, makes the awaiting of "his hour" an essential dimension of his public life.

Now then, is there any difference on this point between fruits that mature in a given time and persons who require

time to mature in liberty? What is it that time does to us
that it plays such an important role?

Time is essential, but not only in its *chronological*, quantitative dimension. *Time is experience*, yes, but only if one
gave oneself the opportunity of *making an experience of experience*. That is: it is not only a matter of things happening, but also appropriating the sense and the message of
the things that happen. Time has meaning within spiritual
activity, in which memory, fantasy, intuition, the ability to
judge come into play. . . . Few have delved into it in a manner as profound and as beautiful as Saint Augustine:

> What, then, is time? If nobody asks me, I know; if I
> want to explain it to somebody who asks me, I do not
> know. [. . .] The past and future, what are they, since
> the past is no longer, and the future is not yet? There
> are three tenses: the present of the past, the present
> of the present, and the present of the future. They ex-
> ist, indeed, in the soul, in a certain way, these three
> modes of time, and I do not see them anywhere else:
> the present of the past is the **memory**; the present of
> the present is **vision**; the present of the future is
> **waiting**.
>
> — *Confessions*, Book XI, (*emphasis added*)

Maturation in time in the human being is much more
than the objective passage of a biological program. It is
the "distension of the soul", Saint Augustine said; that is,
the experience itself of time occurs in the soul itself, in its
movement and activity. Indeed, to mature in time is to put
memory, *vision*, and *waiting* in play. For the absentminded,

for him who does not register what has happened and his own internal events, time is merely a senseless flow. Without memory, we live in a mere present without density, a present that is always beginning, empty. To be immature is, in this regard, just to have always been *recently arrived*, not to have the support of remembered and pondered experiences before the need to give responses to the challenges of reality.

Sometimes we say that we are an immature people. But that is not due to the fact that we have a still brief history, but that *we have not known how to ruminate this history*. We have learned little, and we tend to trip repeatedly over the same stone. Since we do not learn, since we do not trim and modify ourselves based on prior experiences that could teach us a lot, there remains to us only a hollow present, the present of *everything now*, the present of consumerism, squandering, the eagerness for easy money, irresponsibility (anyway, who is going to remember?) or, in an attempt to protect ourselves, the immediate present of mutual mistrust and skepticism.

To call upon memory, to maintain memory open to triumphs and failures, to moments of happiness and moments of suffering, is the only way of not being like *children* in the worst sense of the term: immature, without experience, tremendously vulnerable, victims of whatever colorful lure presents itself to our gaze. Or like *old people* in an even sadder sense: unbelieving, armored in bitterness. *Selective memory* also fails to mature, since it splinters facts, key moments, life episodes, disfiguring the totality. A kind of mythological beast is created: one half lived reality, one half fantasy (whether it be called illusion, ideology, desire). In addition, it is good to remember that the manipulation of memory is never innocent; rather it is dishonest.

And what of waiting, the present of the future in the soul, according to Saint Augustine? How can there be experience and good sense if we do not know where we want to go, in what direction to look in order to choose among the possibilities that present themselves, and in which to sow, to construct, to invest? The temporal dimension of maturity also implies taking account of the *distension* of waiting: *to convert desire into hope.* The present, as a moment of decision, as the only actuality of that liberty which chooses, is diluted without this ability to see what we desire in the minimal movements and the tiny seeds that we have in our hands today. Seeds that we would throw away, movements that we would allow to be lost if we were unable to feed the expectation that beginning with them, and with intervening time and new decisions, the good that we desire and have learned to wait for actively can grow. And thus, Saint Augustine keeps saying, the present is *vision*: of what was, what is and, above all, of what can be. The very domain of liberty, the very domain of the spirit. In this aspect of vision the dimension of complementarity is rooted, a necessary element of maturity.

Without this conjunction of the past, present, and future that occurs in the human soul, no projects are possible. Only improvisation. To erase what happened before in order to begin to write again, without grips or supports, something that will be erased tomorrow. Isn't it about time to learn to project, to wait and to sustain effort and waiting? Let's return to the first point of our reflection: isn't there something of this in the terrible exposure experienced by our children and adolescents? Are they not facing life without a *narrative* that permits them to build their identity and formulate their options? And it is not a matter of returning to the trumpeted and worn-out topic of the end of the story, which was nothing other than the violent imposition of a unique narrative, a *story*, yes, *without time*, based on blind confidence in the laws relating to wealth, the oblivion and the illusion that the avalanche of consumer items was really the promised land. *Narrative* that nobody had ever confirmed, a collective illusion that could only be believed by burying memory and degrading hope. This happens when ideology focuses all human activity and imposes itself with a dogmatism that knows nothing of memory nor of reality nor of vision. The *adolescent progressivism* of today blocks all real human progress and, in the name of a claim of progress but without the force of memory, reality, and vision, configures totalitarian schemes of various types but cruel like those of the twentieth century; totalitarianisms led by *democratic gurus* of monolithic thinking. It confuses the process of maturation of people and countries with a canned milk factory.

Today we have the opportunity to wake up to one of the most horrible consequences of the disorientation of adults: *the death of children*. If there is no past, nothing is learned, if there is no future, nothing is either risked or prepared. We all remain dangling from nothingness, from this lying atemporality of the big screen. Everything today, everything now, what else matters? And the one who did not hit the jackpot lost. And he was lost. He doesn't have a place, he doesn't have time. He will wander through the streets and nobody will see him, like the children begging in swarms or hitting the public phone booth to extract a few cents. Children without time, children who have not been given the time they needed. Or like the adolescents who do not know how to wait and do not have anywhere to learn it, with absent or empty parents, with a society that excludes or expels them and sets them up as victims or victimizers (choosing their gang, oftentimes by the color of their skin) instead of recognizing them as subjects full of a future . . . if and when the community contributes what they need for it.

The same immediatism that has produced adolescents that today, only today, believe that they can satisfy themselves with whatever products are offered today, because it is necessary to sell today, it does not matter if tomorrow the child is alive or not, if he grows or not, if he learns or not. Adolescents who, in the exasperation of the present as the sole horizon, are many times victims or victimizers of or by the compulsion to have a dollar today for whatever and by whatever means, although it be the worst, raffling their lives and that of others because anyway, what does tomorrow matter? Today, only today, to the point of killing in order to have some money, in the same way that older people have accommodated death (or provoked it) in order to have a much larger amount of money.

It is the law of life . . . when there is no *distension of the soul*. When the past is not *memory* and the future is not *waiting*, the present is not *vision* but mortal blindness.

But allow me to conclude with more precision: to take time is not the same as to let oneself be. Vigilance is an essential aspect of waiting. Jesus himself, attentive to his hour, abounded in images which he showered upon his disciples in the parables of the servants waiting for their master, of the virgins who prudently and wisely awaited the bridegroom and those who did not. Here is where we see the potential proper to the present time: *not only vision, but gift.* The present is that which we receive not in order to let it become the past uselessly but in order to convert it into future . . . by acting.

To conclude this section: liberty is fulfilled completely, *maturely*, when it is responsible liberty. It is then that it becomes a point of meeting among the three dimensions of time. A liberty that recognizes what it did and what it did not do (from the present to the past), appropriates its decisions at the corresponding instant (the present) and takes account of the consequences (from the present to the future). That is a mature liberty.

Maturity Implies Liberty

A second dimension of maturity is connected with the *tension between the individual and the community.* A tension, we can indicate from the outset, that at least is inevitable, in the sense that most certainly one cannot exist without the other, and vice versa.

But let us skip over the basic questions implicit in this theme (and sufficiently articulated in biblical anthropology and in the vision of man, a unique person and a social being at the same time) in order to ponder at depth the relation between *being a mature person* (that is to say, according to the second definition of the dictionary, to possess "good judgment or prudence, good sense") and being someone who is *adapted to society*.

In a first and rapid approximation, it would appear that maturity has to do with this *adaptation*. Commonly, at least, it immediately connects the *immature* with the *maladapted*. Sometimes (including in our institutions), the concept of *immaturity* serves to stigmatize without morally condemning the one who steps outside of *the expected*, who acts in a way that is surprising or inappropriate by popular standards. "He isn't a bad person, just a bit immature." Is that not a way of talking that is quite usual among us? The problem with this is twofold. In the first place, it is not relevant to speak about an immature person, but of immature conduct. And even so, it is not so easy to define the standard that discriminates one conduct from the other. Who defines what is *mature*, that is to say, what one has *to adapt himself* to? Is it *the authorities*? The *majority*? The *established*?

The standard that assimilates maturity to adaptation becomes particularly complicated if we take certain situations as examples. Not so long ago, the authorities of our country said that "silence is health" and made it stick. Nevertheless, individuals were not lacking who raised their voices in favor of human rights and against the various abuses of the poor and those who did not swallow the dominant ideology. Another example: probably, the majority considers it more adapted to the world in which we live to make a little gift to the transit agent or the inspector than to pay a considerable fine in the relevant office. Is it a question of *immaturity* to refuse to enter this net of corruption, no less pernicious for being *accepted*? But of course, the specter of established practice appears here, in this case, the transport law, or the regulation over the legal permits for large or small shops. Although many Argentines would chafe, the adapted (and mature) would not be on the side of corrupt but widespread practices but on the side of what the law requires, although it is little followed. And yet, things become complicated when individuals are obliged to act against the law in the name of what they consider just. It is the history of the workers movement all over the world: how much fighting, how much suffering, even how many deaths, were the price of recognizing the legitimacy of the protection of the worker and his family, of the regulation of the work of minors, and so forth, against the rapacity of the capitalism of the era, which had generated its own legality? Could it be said that those pioneers in the struggle for the dignity of human labor were *immature persons*?

We Christians ought to be the first (and we are not always!) to reject the hasty identification between *maturity* and *adaptation*. No less a personage than Jesus could have been seen by many of his time as the paradigm of the maladapted, and thus, as immature. The evangelists themselves witness to this when recording the reactions to his practices ("Behold, a glutton and a drunkard, a friend of tax collectors and sinners!" Mt 11:19) and his ruptures with institutional frameworks ("And when his friends heard it, they went out to seize him, for they said, 'He is beside himself'", Mk 3:21, and the reply of Jesus regarding his *true family*, Mk 3:33–35). The same is implied in his polemic with the Pharisees and the high priests regarding the Law and the temple. We could read all the Gospels, and particularly that of John, as the attempt to respond to this question directed to the Lord: "By what authority are you doing these things, or who gave you this authority to do them?" (Mk 11:28). At that time, when there was neither a scientific mentality nor even a humanistic one in the modern sense, one who in some way defied authority, institutional or majoritarian, was not considered *immature*, but rather having "a demon" (Jn 8:48–52) or engaging in "blasphemy" (Jn 10:33). Thus, the reaction to Jesus' attitude would culminate in the mortal accusations of blasphemy in the first place (Mt 26:65–66) and then of rebellion against Caesar (Jn 19:12–15).

And what to say about Saint Peter, an undesirable for the *establishment* in so many situations, to the point of prison, stoning and finally, execution? And so many martyrs and confessors, confronting the standards and values of their time, calling down upon themselves the ire of those in power? Well considered, the saints have always been like a pebble in the shoe of their contemporaries. And it could not be otherwise, taking account of the source of the authority of Jesus, which transcends all the good judgment that is possible in this world.

If maturity were adaptation, smoothly and fully, the end of our educational task would be to *adapt* the children, these anarchic creatures, to the good norms of society, whatever they were. At what cost? At the cost of the muzzling and submission of the conscience. Or, even worse, at the cost of the deprivation of that which is essential and sacred to the person: his liberty. A tremendous challenge, then, *education in and for liberty*, since it assumes in all of us, educators and trainers, pastors and teachers, a self-effacing relativization of our way of seeing and feeling in order to dispose ourselves to the humble and sincere search for the truth.

By an indirect path, then, we come to see that maturity implies, more than the adaptation to a reigning model, the ability to take a position of one's own in a given situation in which one finds oneself. That is to say, the possession of the freedom to choose and to decide according to one's own experience and desire, consistent with one's values.

Maturity Is Made Complete in Love

Now, does this mean the automatic canonization of subjectivism, of all eccentricity, of every pretension of the individual as such?

By no means. The question that his contemporaries asked Jesus was in itself valid. His words and works could not present themselves as a rupture: they had to have a reference to truth. The *negative* moment of criticism, of rebellion, of subjectivity as a rejection of restraint, can only sustain itself in the *positive moment of transcendence, of the tendency toward a greater universality, to a fuller truth*. It is not power that the martyrs rejected: it was power that benefited only some. It was not the Law that Jesus combated: it was the Law that placed itself above the recognition of the neighbor. It is not the majority that the witness of the truth rejects: it is the majority insofar as it deprives other presences and other voices of visibility and words.

In other words: liberty is not an end in itself, a black hole behind which there is nothing. It is ordered to the fuller life of the human being, of every man and of all men. It is governed by love, as an unconditional affirmation of life, and the value of all and of each one. In this sense, we can take a further step in our reflection: maturity does not imply the ability to decide freely, to be subject to one's own options in the middle of multiple situations and historical configurations in which we may see ourselves included, but it includes the full affirmation of love as the bond between human beings. In the different ways in which this bond occurs: interpersonal, intimate, social, political, intellectual. . . .

It is nothing other than the idea we have presented of a *responsible liberty*. Before whom are we going to be responsible, if not before the other and before ourselves as members of the human family? Stop, you will say. Are we not responsible, first of all, before God? Yes, of course. It is certain that we see God as if through a mirror darkly, an enigma. . . . And the most definitive proof of the veracity and the truth of our responsibility before him continues to be the proof of love toward the neighbor (1 Jn 4:20), lived from the most intimate truth of our conscience (1 Jn 3:21–24) to the most concrete and effective work that shows our faith (Jas 2:18). A *mature personality*, thus, *is that which has succeeded in inserting its unique and unrepeatable character upon the community of his fellow men*. The difference is not enough: *it is necessary also to recognize the similarity*.

What does this imply for our vocation and task as Christian teachers?

It implies the necessity of *constructing and reconstructing the social and communitarian ties that unrestrained indi-*

vidualism has broken. A society, a people, a community, is not just the sum of individuals who leave each other alone. The negative definition of liberty, which claims that it ends where the other begins, goes only half way. Why do I want a liberty that encloses me in the cell of my individuality, that leaves others outside, that prevents me from opening the door and sharing with the neighbor? What type of desirable society is that where each one enjoys his goods in solitude, and for which the other is a potential enemy until he demonstrates to me that he has no interest in me?

I would like to be thoroughly understood: Christians are not those who are going to fall into a romantic and naïve conception of human nature. Beyond historical formulations, the belief in original sin accounts for the fact that in every man or woman there dwells an immense capacity for good . . . and for evil. No one is immune, in every fellow man there can also dwell the worst enemy, even for himself.

But that consideration, realist or theological, as you will, is only the beginning. Because from there it is necessary to think about what the task of man in history, the enterprise of human communities, the finality of civilization, consist of: simply sanctioning the dangerousness of one against another limiting the possibilities of conflict, or rather promoting the highest human abilities in the order of a growth of communion, love and mutual recognition that aims at the construction of a positive link and not simply a negative one?

We have advanced much, and a great deal remains still to advance, in the task of bringing to light the numerous situations of violation of the dignity of persons, and especially, of the most penalized and subjugated. Particularly important has been the advance in the consciousness of the rights of children, along with the rights of men and women, of the equality of rights of minorities. But it is necessary to take a further step: *it will not be through the exalting of individualism that the rights of the person will be given their proper place.* The ultimate right of a person is not only that no one impedes him from achieving his ends, but that he effectively achieves them. It is not enough to avoid injustice, if justice is not promoted. It is not enough to protect children from negligence, abuse and maltreatment if young people are not educated for a full and integral love for their future children. If resources are not made available to families of every kind that they need in order to fulfill their indispensable mission. If a whole attitude of welcome and love for the life of all and of every one of its members is not favored in society through the different means to which the state must contribute.

A mature person, a mature society, then, will be that whose liberty is fully responsible from love. And that does not grow by itself on the shoulder of the road. It implies investing a lot of work, a lot of patience, much sincerity, much humility, much magnanimity.

Walking toward Maturity

How can we convert these reflections into *concrete avenues* for Christian educators to put into effect the tasks which are urgently demanded of us?

To Strengthen the Ecclesial Community

In the first place, I believe that it is crucial to *reinforce the ecclesial sense among ourselves*. There is no other place to incline our ear to what God tells us at the present time but in the bosom of the believing community. The humble ecclesial community, real and concrete, not the desired or dreamed-of version. With its lacks and sins, in the course of a process of penitence and conversion, never completed, seeking new and better paths of mutual communication, of fraternal correction, of solidarity, of growth in fidelity and wisdom. . . . It is possible that many Christians, in the face of the painful divisions and sins which the ecclesial body is enduring, will be discouraged and seek the paths for realizing their commitment to their neighbor outside of the community. But perhaps in so doing they may be deprived of the richness which they will be able to find only in the believing community. We do not all think the same way, and sometimes the differences appear irreconcilable. We do not all act the way we should, nor do we all carry fully into practice the Word which we experience. But that ought not to be an obstacle to continue praying, dialoguing, working so that that Word may be incarnate and shine before everyone. Perhaps the first pledge, the first search, should be that of *making a reality of an ecclesial community that is much more respectful of the neighbor, less prejudiced, and more mature in the faith, in love, and in service.*

To Try New Forms of Dialogue in a Pluralist Society

In the second place, to create a sense of responsible freedom in love in the *relations among distinct groups that make up our society.* This is a particularly important task for us, in that the social and cultural changes that we are seeing in our country, as already seen in other parts of the world, place before us *the need of finding new forms of dialogue and coexistence in a pluralist society*, through which differences *come to be accepted and respected, and to strengthen the spaces and topics of meeting and concord.* How many Christians work shoulder to shoulder with brothers of other confessions and religious groups, or of political and social movements, in the tasks of human advancement and service to the needy! Perhaps a new way of relating is gestating there, that will help to reconstruct the social bond among Argentines and to amplify our consciousness of solidarity beyond every religious, ideological, and political frontier.

To Revitalize the Specifically Theological Dimension of Our Motivation

In the third place, I would like to briefly note the highest dimension of maturity, which is *sanctity.* If all of this reflection does not move us as Christians *to recommit over and over to the ultimate motivation of our existence*, we will have gotten stuck only at the halfway point. For the Christian, action of liberty in time is accomplished according to the *eucharistic model*: the proclamation of salvation effected today in Christ and in each one through faith (with words and deeds), which *fulfills the past history of salvation and anticipates* the definitive future. Hope in its fullest theological sense thus becomes the key of Christian expression in time, centered in the adherence of the person to the Resurrected One.

It is relevant in this regard to keep very much in mind what the Holy Father indicates in *Mane Nobiscum Domine*: "The Eucharist not only provides the interior strength needed for this mission, but is also—in some sense—*its plan*. For the Eucharist is a mode of being, which passes from Jesus into each Christian, through whose testimony it is meant to spread throughout society and culture. For this to happen, each member of the faithful must assimilate, through personal and communal meditation, the values which the Eucharist expresses, the attitudes it inspires, the resolutions to which it gives rise. Can we not see here *a special charge* which could emerge from this *Year of the Eucharist?*" (n. 25)

And all that in the heart of the community that shares faith rooted in love. Because overcoming the contradiction between the individual and society is never completed, from our point of view, in a mere search for consensus, but it has to *ascend toward the source of all truth*. To deepen dialogue in order to yield more fully to the truth, deepening our truths in a dialogue that not we but God initiates, and that has its own time and its own pedagogy. A dialogue that is a *path toward truth together*.

To Establish Concrete Educational Goals toward Maturity

To conclude, and placing ourselves in the specific task of the educator, we have to try to make the central point of our activities the integral formation of the person, that is to say, the contribution to the full maturation of free and responsible men and women. In this sense, we would need to be able to propose concrete goals that can be evaluated, in order not to remain in narcissistic rhetoric. With your permission, I would not like to conclude without suggesting some questions derived from the preceding reflection, that could mobilize some in practice, others in objectives, others even in content that cuts across these categories. Here are six proposals:

Awaken Memory in Order to "Experience the Experience"

The absence of historical memory is a serious defect of our society. What is more, it is a distinctive note of the culture some refer to as *postmodern*, the juvenile culture of *that was then*. All reference to history is seen as a merely academic question, in the most sterile sense of the word *history*. I believe it is essential to awaken in our children the ability to connect with the motivations, options and actions of those who preceded them, discovering the undeniable relation between them and the present. To know and to be able to take a position vis-à-vis past events is the only possibility for constructing a future with meaning. And this must be not only the content of a specific subject matter, but must cut across the entirety of scholarly life through various activities and in distinct arenas. In this sense, contact with the *classics* of literature, meetings at the metahistorical dimension of the social life of the people, are critical.

Helping to Live the Present as Gift

If God comes out to meet us in concrete history, the present is the point from which we embrace the gift and give our response. This implies transcending the skepticism which today has set up camp in our culture, and also to go beyond certain typically Argentine delusions of grandeur. To live the present as a gift is to receive it with humility and put it to productive work. In the message that I offered you two years ago I developed the theme of the relation between continuity and innovation in historical creation. I invite you to take it up once more and to find ways of generating enthusiasm in our young people for the enormous transformative potential that lies in their grasp, not so much through harangues and discourses but rather bringing them together to develop experiences and concrete situations that permit them to discover their own abilities.

Developing the Capacity of Critical Judgment in Order to Escape the "Dictatorship of Opinion"

Let us not tire of asking ourselves over and over if we are not simply transmitting information instead of educating for liberty, which requires the ability to understand and critique situations and discourses. If we live ever more in an *information society* that saturates us with indiscriminate data, all at the same level, school ought to protect its role of teaching to think, and to think critically. To do this, we teachers have to be able to show the reasons that underlie the different options for reading reality as well as promote the practice of listening to all voices before issuing judgments. Additionally, we will have to help to establish evaluative standards and, as the last step which is not always taken into account, bring out how all judgment should leave room for follow-up questions, avoiding the risk of positing absolutes and rapidly losing vitality.

Accepting and Integrating One's Own Corporal Reality

Of particular urgency is the acceptance and integration of man's corporality. Paradoxically, present-day culture places the body at the center of its discourse and at the same time subjects it to all kinds of constrictions and demands. An anthropology that was more attentive to the new conditions of subjectivity cannot ignore concrete work on this point, from all the spheres in which it is problematic (health, image and identity, sexuality, sport, well-being and leisure, work), and always pointing toward an integral liberation for love of self, the other and God.

Deepening Social Values

We know that our young people have an enormous capacity to feel the suffering of their neighbor and to give themselves body and soul to common action. This social sensibility, often merely emotional, should be educated toward a solidarity of *depth*, that can thoughtfully elaborate the relationship between evidently painful and unjust situations, and discourses and practices which give rise to them and perpetuate them. It is by starting with a permanent *back-and-forth* among experiences of authentic human encounter and their illumination originating in the gospel that we must reconstruct the values of solidarity and of meaning of the collective, that the consumer and competitive individualism of recent times have undermined in our country. Doubtless, this will require a deepening and renovating of social doctrine in our concrete context.

Insisting on Preaching the Kerygma

All the above will fall through the cracks if we do not accompany our young people in a journey of personal conversion to the person and message of Jesus, with ultimate motivation that articulates the other aspects. This will require of us, in addition to personal coherence—there is no preaching possible without testimony—an open and sincere search for the forms that religious experience can take in our century. Conversion, dear brothers, is not something that happens once and for all. It is to adore God "in Spirit and truth", that is to say, wherever this spirit blows.

Argentina Awaken . . .

We arrive thus at the end of our meditation.

We find ourselves in an historical moment of sorrow and of hope. We feel that we cannot *respond with indifference* in the face of the opportunity that providence offers us to contribute our bricks to the construction of a different world.

With sorrow we have shared the confirmation of the suffering and abandonment experienced by so many of our children, expressed in a tragic manner in some events of the past year, and we have recognized the *necessity of responding to this situation*, of taking responsibility in some way, from our poverty but also from our hope.

And in this context, we have reflected about the conditions of personal and collective maturity required for this commitment.

Maturity that implies a capacity to live time as memory, as vision and as waiting, going beyond immediacy in order to be able to articulate the best of our memory and of our desires in effective and thoughtful action.

Maturity that is displayed in a liberty that is not subject to an exclusive particularity, that turns a deaf ear to half-truths and cardboard horizons, that does not adapt uncritically to what is current nor criticizes simply as a projection of individuality, but that points the way in the *search for universal and efficacious love that provides a foundation and gives content to this fully responsible liberty.*

And which leads, in the end, to a *renewed life of ecclesial faith and of facing society as a whole*, well founded in a *theological and Eucharistic experience.*

Whence I proposed to you six goals for work with the children: to awaken the *memory*; to help them to live the *present as a gift*; to develop the capacity for *critical judgment*; to encourage the acceptance and integration of their own *corporeal reality*; to deepen *social values*, and to insist on the preaching of the *kerygma*.

If the reality that challenges us today finds in us a generous and valiant spirit, the present moment will also have been a gift of growth for us. It will be thus that the personal and communitarian maturity of our educational communities will have transcended itself, by the grace of God, toward an experience with him in a life of sanctity, the response to a gift which precedes and envelops us, a sign and anticipation in history of the fullness for which we wait and hope.

I take my leave from you appropriating the words of the Apostle: "Therefore, my beloved brethren, be steadfast, immovable, always abounding in the work of the Lord, knowing that in the Lord your labor is not in vain." (1 Cor 15:58) And, please, I ask you to pray for me.

— Buenos Aires, at Easter,
in the year of our Lord 2005

Key to Reading
for Working Individually or in Groups

🖊 Let's reflect

"We have the sensation that *Providence has given us a new opportunity* to establish ourselves in a truly just and supportive community, where all persons are respected in their dignity and promoted in their liberty, in order to fulfill their destiny as daughters and sons of God.

"This opportunity is also a challenge. We have in our hands an immense responsibility, derived precisely from the requirement not to squander the chance that has been offered to us. It is not possible to incline one's ear to the Word of salvation outside the place where it sets out for this encounter with us, that is, in the concrete *human history* in which the Lord became incarnate."

FOR PERSONAL REFLECTION

—Does my faith life impel me to form community or is it reduced to an individual experience?

—What are my deficiencies of liberty?

—Do I have a passive attitude before Providence?

FOR WORK IN GROUPS

—What signs of maturity do we see in our Church?

—What emerging values do we find in our society?

—What steps can we take in order to encourage respect and liberty in our generation?

⌁ Let's read

"Now when Jesus heard this, he withdrew from there in a boat to a lonely place apart. But when the crowds heard it, they followed him on foot from the towns. As he went ashore he saw a great throng; and he had compassion on them, and healed their sick. When it was evening, the disciples came to him and said, 'This is a lonely place, and the day is now over; send the crowds away to go into the villages and buy food for themselves.' Jesus said, 'They need not go away; you give them something to eat.' They said to him, 'We have only five loaves here and two fish.' And he said, 'Bring them here to me.' "

—Matthew 14:13–18

⌁ Let's think

The Catholic school has as its specific duty the complete Christian formation of its pupils, and this task is of special significance today because of the inadequacy of the family and society. It knows that this integration of faith and life is part of a life-long process of conversion until the pupil becomes what God wishes him to be. Young people have to be taught to share their personal lives with God. They are to overcome their individualism and discover, in the light of faith, their specific vocation to live responsibly in a community with others. The very pattern of the Christian life draws them to commit themselves to serve God in their brethren and to make the world a better place for man to live in.

—*The Catholic School, 45*

◢ Let's review our task

As Christian educators we propose not only to transmit knowledge but also to form *mature persons*. In this sense, maturity could be understood as the *ability to use our liberty in a sensible, prudent manner.*

In other words, it is a question of teaching our children and adolescents that the present is that which we receive not in order to allow it uselessly to become the past, but rather to convert it into the future by acting.

A mature personality is that which has managed to insert his unique and unrepeatable character into the community of his fellows. Difference is not enough: it is also necessary to recognize the similarity.

How can we convert these reflections into concrete pathways so that we as Christian educators can put into motion these urgent tasks which are demanded of us?

Let us together think about three actions which put into practice the following objectives:

—To strengthen the ecclesial community.

—To try new forms of dialogue in a pluralist society.

—To revitalize the specifically theological dimension of our motivation.

—To establish concrete educational goals for maturity.

✎ **Let us pray**

> Mary, Virgin of hearing
> and of the Word made flesh in your womb,
> help us to be receptive
> to the word of the Lord,
> so that, welcomed and meditated,
> it may grow in our heart.
> Help us to live, like you,
> the bliss of believers
> and to dedicate ourselves with untiring love
> to the evangelization of those who seek
> your Son.
>
> —*John Paul II*

Words of John Paul II
to Christian Educators

God has entrusted to you the singular task of guiding young people along the path of sanctity. Be for them an example of faithful generosity to Christ. Encourage them not to hesitate to *put out into the deep*, responding without delay to the invitation of the Lord.

He calls some to family life, others to consecrated life or to sacerdotal ministry. Help them to be able to discern which is their path, and to be true friends of Christ and authentic disciples.

When believing adults make the face of Christ visible with words and example, young people are more easily willing to receive their demanding message marked by the mystery of the Cross.

Most Holy Virgin, Mother of the Redeemer, sure guide on the path toward God and fellow man, who kept his words in the depths of your heart, protect with maternal intercession families and Christian communities, so that they may help adolescents and young people to respond generously to the call of the Lord. *Amen.*